MARKETING FOR FINANCIAL ADVICE PROFESSIONALS

MARKETING FOR FINANCIAL ADVICE PROFESSIONALS

Proven Tips and Techniques to Attract More of your Dream Clients in the Digital Age

By Philip Calvert

ISBN: 979-8-61-023715-2

ACKNOWLEDGEMENTS

For the tens of thousands of IFAs, Advisers and Financial Planners I've met in the UK and around the world over the last forty-two years in their offices, at industry conferences, workshops and online.

In particular I would like to mention Bryn Jones, Tom Cameron, Clive Greig, Paul Rutherford and Dennis Kent at National Employers Life (NEL) for showing me the ropes.

And at Zurich Life, Clive Waller and Russell Fryer for showing me where the best pubs were.

Thanks also to other key people who I have looked up to, such as Roland Rawicz-Szczerbo, Donald Birts, Nick Bamford, Jacqui Harper MBE, Thomas Power, Penny Power MBE, John Macpherson, Russell Brunson, Allan Pease and the incredible Osmond D Rockcliffe – who was the single best dressed man in financial advice.

Join our Free Private Facebook Group for Financial Advisers, IFAs and Financial Planners

Network with your peers, share ideas and best practice and get answers to your business development and technical questions.

And get a **free** Social Media Strategy Planner for Financial Advice businesses – including a ready-made *Value Based Social Media Strategy* for IFAs, financial planners and advisers.

Request your invitation and free eBook by sending a message to philip@financialadvice.marketing quoting reference: GP2020

CONTENTS

- Love local
- Love junk
- Out and about
- Add to home screen
- Feel the love
- I saw this and thought of you
- Red carpet treatment

Take it Personally

Keeping the Plates Spinning

Keep it Professional

A Powerhouse of Opportunity

Kittens in Boxes

Hide and Seek

Playing by the Rules

The Dream 100

Greetings with a Twist

At the checkout

PS

About the author

Disclaimer and Terms of Use

INTRODUCTION

It turned out that pension scheme administration was not really for me, and Bryn Jones - my boss at NEL (National Employers Life) in Dorking, Surrey suggested that I might prefer sales. That role was promoting our products to brokers and financial advisers, in the hope that they, in turn would recommend them to their clients.

A good pay rise, bonus scheme and brand-new bright red company Ford Escort later, I left the leafy Dorking countryside and headed for the metropolis that was Croydon, where I was assigned Surrey and the South West of London as my patch. I distinctly remember driving away from NEL's head office Milton Court with Gloria Gaynor's *I Will Survive* playing loudly on the car stereo. It was Spring 1979.

On arriving on my first day at Leon House in Croydon, my new boss Tom Cameron introduced me to my fellow Broker Consultants (we were called Life Inspectors then) and talked me through the financial advisers on my patch, which stretched from Brixton in the east to Bracknell in the west and south down to Guildford.

Within that area were literally hundreds of financial advice firms. These varied from small general insurance brokers who did a little life, pensions, mortgage and protection business, through to quality 'IFAs' as we might know them today. There were also some large accountancy businesses that offered financial advice and several large national firms operating mostly in the employee benefits sphere. 'Financial Planning' didn't really exist - it was mostly just broking.

In fact, Financial Planning was not a concept or phrase that I ever heard used. The industry was fundamentally about selling financial products to clients and for the most part, despite scandals and mis-selling that were to come later, clients, advisers and product providers generally lived in harmony.

Advisers were paid commission – a type of remuneration which was to come under close scrutiny later, and back then provider golf days and trips overseas were commonplace. A few years later I got a rap on the knuckles (but also a quietly spoken *"Well done Philip"*) from my boss for notching up the most expensive business lunch for a broker in the company's history. That lunch also resulted in me winning a £2 million key man policy from one of the most successful financial advisers in the City. We won it on rate, of course...

Today, none of that would be allowed, and rightly so – but back in the day, barely a day went by without taking a broker out for lunch. Relationships with brokers also worked both ways, with strong friendships often developing between advisers and Broker Consultants. I know several of my colleagues at NEL and later Zurich Life who became Best Men at advisers' weddings.

I vividly remember a day when a financial adviser in Surrey ordered me to take off the afternoon so that he could buy me lunch as a thank you for helping them out with sales and marketing ideas. We ended up in a pub near to where the Benny Hill Show was being filmed, and at

2pm the entire cast and crew piled in for 'refreshment'. You can guess the rest…

Sales training was also a big deal at the time, with incredibly expensive sales experts regularly being hired by providers to train both their broker consultants and financial advisers.

I remember my very first meeting with a financial adviser. I had completed my training and the meeting was at his home in Weybridge. At the time he was with Hambro Life, which soon after became Allied Dunbar. My company NEL was known for being big players in the PHI (Permanent Health Insurance) market – a product that paid a replacement income in the event that the policy holder couldn't do their job because of sickness or accident. It was vital then, and its modern counterpart still is.

The Hambro adviser that I was meeting (let's call him Mark) was a big fan of these policies because as he said at the time *"Literally everyone needs one"*, but Hambro didn't offer the product, so we were able to offer him and other advisers an agency to sell our own products.

My meeting with him was to assess his suitability to have an agency with us, highlight the commission options, get him to complete the agency application forms, drop off some brochures, go through some sales ideas and then take him to the pub.

As it turned out Mark was way ahead of me in terms of sales ideas. My patch had been vacant for a few months and all he needed to get started selling our products was an official visit from me to sign him off. But while he had been waiting, he had already planned how he was going to sell the product. In fact, he was a very professional guy, with some quality clients – such as dentists, doctors, accountants and solicitors.

After we had completed the agency application forms, I started my presentation on how he could sell the products. This was my big moment.

I was thirty seconds into my presentation when Mark said *"Philip, stop."*.

Then he added *"Let me show you how to make a sales presentation."* Mark was, after all, a successful consultant with Hambro Life, and who had been through what many people at the time agreed was the best training in the industry. If you were ever trained at Hambro, you will know what I mean.

There and then, in his smart home office in Weybridge, Mark showed me how to use a note pad and pen to engage the prospect. He taught me how to sell through drawing shapes and lines *upside down* on the pad – and how to keep eye contact with the prospect by raising and lowering the pen.

He taught me the importance of telling stories through drawing, so as to ensure the message was not just heard, but also seen in a graphic form. He told me that having the skill of writing and drawing upside down was vital because the prospect could see everything, even when sitting opposite each other across a table.

There I was at the age of nineteen at my first business meeting. I was quite simply entranced by what I was hearing and seeing, and it all seemed to make a lot of sense. Ever since then I have been fascinated by the art and psychology of storytelling in sales and marketing and have consumed multiple volumes on the subject.

There was also a time when telephone selling and body language were all important within the industry, and I eagerly snapped up any training that was available. In the process I met some of the giants of sales training from around the world, including the amazing Allan Pease from Australia, who was renowned for his courses on cold calling and latterly body language expertise. Allan was at one time, the most successful life assurance salesman at the youngest age and went on to be one of the world's top speakers and trainers.

Mark and I got on very well, and over the next few years he put a great deal of PHI business our way, and I remember having conversations with my boss about how we dreaded the day when Allied Dunbar would launch their own PHI product.

A Dirty Word

Sales went on to become a dirty word within the world of financial advice, and from around 1992 onwards was barely uttered. But fast-forward to today, and even the most highly regarded and respected financial planners talk about the importance of sales – to be precise, selling the concept and importance of financial planning and articulating their value.

And this is important, because for the most part, product sales are increasingly being replaced by financial planning sales – a subtle but very important difference.

Financial advisers are also working hard on building trust, yet this is not necessarily the complete answer to enhancing the perception of the industry as a profession.

In February 2018, industry expert Phil Young of Zero Support published an article in Money Marketing titled *The Trust Paradox in Financial Services - What is driving more people into the arms of individuals and businesses they purportedly do not trust?*

The article began:

The financial services industry does not suffer from a lack of trust. If anything, it has enjoyed a surfeit of it. Almost every scandal involves someone handing over money they could not afford to lose into the hands of someone they trust – be it an individual or a large corporate.

My family understands this only too well, with my own mother (a former magistrate) being defrauded out of her entire savings by what she thought was her bank.

Phil ends his article:

Perhaps trust is a problem, but it only appears to be so with hindsight, long after the horse has bolted. I have seen plenty of survey responses from highly satisfied customers of businesses who have been quietly ripping them off for years.

Ignorance is a blissfully satisfied customer. Trust is an emotion – not a fact – and we frequently conflate it with customer satisfaction. When you look at behaviour rather than survey responses, it suggests to me the problem is not consumer trust but industry ethics. A new perspective is required.

I look back at my forty+ year career with fondness, and whilst much has improved for the better in terms of ethics, regulation and professionalism, I still meet hundreds of high quality financial advisers every year who are looking for new ways to highlight their expertise, promote their services and articulate their value.

In my early days, *highlighting their expertise and promoting their services* was the last thing they wanted, because back then it was all about **sales ideas** to sell products, and we as providers would spend a huge amount of time and money helping them to do just that.

But thankfully times have changed, s*ales* is not a dirty word and we can now help financial advisers with ideas to:

- Highlight and promote their expertise
- Highlight and promote their professionalism
- Highlight and promote their technical excellence
- Highlight and promote their knowledge of niche markets
- Highlight and promote their commitment to excellence in customer service
- Highlight and sell their expertise, professionalism and technical excellence in new formats for the digital era – such as eBooks, training courses and webinars

A financial adviser discovering this book in 2020 and beyond might be forgiven for thinking that it will inevitably be full of ideas that make use of social media and digital technology. Yes, it goes without saying that cutting edge ideas are included, but I hope you will be excited to discover some of the most deliciously old-school ideas which have been brought right up to date and applied to the important business of promoting and selling the concept of professional financial planning.

You might also be forgiven for thinking that there will be a chapter on purchasing leads and enquiries via a number of well-known industry websites and services, but I want to avoid that like the plague. My research with thousands of financial advisers suggests that whilst these services have their place, they are predominantly there to support and complement *your own* marketing initiatives. Indeed, many IFAs and advisers have told me that they use such services to 'top up' enquiries as and when needed.

Neither should you expect this book to be an academic tome on marketing. What follows are sales and marketing ideas that I have seen being used by some of the most professional and successful financial advisers and planners around the world. Some take some work and effort, whilst others are ridiculously simple.

You may have heard of some of the ideas here before. You may even have tried and dismissed them in the past, but what I would urge is that you keep an open mind because I have updated them for today's marketplace.

This book will not write your marketing plan for you, because every financial advice firm is different. But it will help you to think more strategically and to give you a lot more focus. This book does what it says on the tin and includes a wealth of ideas that could sit within your own marketing strategy.

Forty years of working with financial advisers has taught me that most firms just want some good, straight-forward ideas that they can try out.

Every adviser firm is different, so employ the ideas that you feel are most appropriate for your own marketplace. But what I have tried to do is write them in such a way that everything included can be used directly as advised or modified to suit your target clients and business plan.

Let's get stuck in...

Just how much business have you missed out on?

Being mindful of the fact that financial advisers from both large and very small firms will be reading this, I've tried hard to make sure that there is something for everyone. Regardless of your role within your business, everything here can work for every reader.

But how much business are you already leaving on the table from a variety of sources?

As we will discover later in more detail, the biggest single leak of enquiries comes from your own website, with our research showing that a terrifying number of your website visitors are leaving without a second glance. Some of these website visitors are your ideal, dream clients. Not all by a long shot, but some of them.

A consistent theme I have discovered over the years with financial advisers is that there is often a kind of assumption that just having a website is automatically going to attract new clients. And that's something I address head-on later. But it's not just your website – there are a multitude of other marketing opportunities that we are missing out on, with potential clients knocking on our doors but going unanswered.

Take LinkedIn for example, consider a few simple questions:

- How many people looked at your profile last week?

- How many people who looked at your profile have you thanked for dropping by?
- How many connections have you thanked for connecting?
- How many of those new connections did you follow up a month later?
- How many new followers have you thanked for following you?
- How many of those new followers did you follow up a month later?
- How many people have you thanked for liking, commenting or sharing your posts or articles?
- How many people have you thanked for liking, commenting or sharing your posts in groups?

How many of those messages could have resulted in a conversation that led somewhere like a phone call, Skype/Zoom meeting or even a coffee shop?

As we'll discover later, I know many financial advisers and other businesspeople who have attracted new clients the very first time they thanked or followed up someone on LinkedIn.

We could ask similar questions based round your Facebook, Twitter, Instagram or YouTube accounts, but the simple fact is there are multiple opportunities to engage with people that we are failing to spot. There was a time when a new client opportunity was all too easy to see:

- A phone call enquiring about our services
- A letter in the post
- Someone giving us a business card at an event
- Someone walking into our office off the street
- Someone asking for a meeting after our seminar

- An email
- Etc.

Today, there are other, less obvious interactions that happen (usually online) which could still lead to someone making an enquiry. And some of those less obvious interactions may well have come about as a result of someone being referred to us by an existing client, but we missed them because we weren't paying attention.

It is critical that we don't just see genuine enquiries as those that come through traditional routes and open our eyes to the fact that some of our potentially best clients will approach us in an unexpected way. And I have personal experience of this having missed out on a couple of speaking enquiries that came through the Facebook Messenger app in the 'Message Requests' tab – the tab which many of us associate with spam from people we're not connected to.

As much as anything else, this book is about opening our minds and opening our eyes. Marketing isn't always about social media; there are many powerful old-school techniques that when combined with digital ideas within the context of a carefully thought-through plan, can produce exciting results.

So let's now look at a multitude of different elements that could form part of our marketing plan. Yes, each idea could result in new client enquiries in its own right, but as you read this book, always aim to be thinking about how you could combine individual elements in a strategy that will make you irresistible to your ideal client.

From Cardboard to Gold

Business Cards

So let's start with the most basic of marketing tools – the humble business card. There are people who will tell you that the business card is dead, and that's just nonsense. Despite the fact that LinkedIn has built a 'business card killer' into its mobile app, your business card is still very important.

However, over my forty-one years working with financial advisers, I have collected an impressive array of business cards. I have kept every single card that I have ever been given at meetings, training events and conferences around the world.

And much to my wife's annoyance they can be found in drawers, cabinets, box files and plastic storage boxes everywhere around our house, office and garage. I have tens of thousands of them.

My wife was an IFA when I met her, and I tell her that I can't throw them out *"…because her own business card is in there somewhere and it would be terrible to lose it…"*

But with such a large collection, comes a great deal of insight into financial advisers' business cards. Here are a few things which consistently stand out:

- Many financial advisers, including very high-end firms are still using Hotmail or BTinternet email addresses

- Many advisers using info@ email addresses instead of their own name

- The text on the cards is far too small

- Many advisers' cards just look cheap and create the wrong impression

- Cards that have a fold in them or open out like an Origami model really are just annoying

- Cards that have gold text or gold edging look ostentatious and create entirely the wrong impression

- Black glossy business cards are hideous

- Glossy business cards look cheap

- Embossed or raised text with 'spot gloss' look fantastic

- Plastic, wooden, rubber, metal or see-through business cards are fun, but don't always add anything to a financial adviser's branding. I've seen them all.

That said, I have one business card from an adviser which is metal and also acts as a cheese grater. He had them made as a client gift at a seminar he was running. I have also seen an adviser's business card which can be put on end in a saucer of water and cress seeds grow out the other end!

An adviser in Canada has a business card where the sides and bottom are normal, but the top edge is jagged like an investment return graph.

I've met another adviser who is well-known in the cycling community, and who has metal business cards with various tools cut into it, such as wheel spanners.

I have seen another financial adviser who gives out a small LEGO piece of a man with his name and phone number on.

And one of my favourites is an IFA in the UK who used to work with footballers, and her business card is green and designed like a football pitch with lines, centre circle etc.

- Many look 'home designed' using an online service. There is still much value to be gained by using a professional designer and printer; they are worth the money

- About ten per cent of business cards still don't have a website address on them

- Hardly any include an adviser's social media links – in particular their LinkedIn URL

One great thing that LinkedIn has done, is to give every user/member their own unique QR code (Quick Response Code).

We've all seen QR codes before and they can be printed on the back of your business card. Everyone knows that they need to be scanned, and these days you don't even need a special QR reader/scanner because on most modern phones you just point your camera at the code.

Simply go to your LinkedIn mobile app, download your personal QR code and print it on either the back or front of your business card.

If nothing else, it will be a talking point when people see it on your card and they will ask you what it is. When they scan it with their phone camera it will take them straight to your LinkedIn profile.

Try scanning the QR code below to see where it takes you...

Another thing you can do, is to include a general QR code on your business card, which when scanned gives people the opportunity to automatically add the contact details to their phone's address book and contacts. Much more on how to use QR codes in your marketing in the next chapter.

In short, without going over the top, try to be imaginative in the design of your business card, and above all don't try and do it on the cheap. A great business card is well worth spending the money on and something to be proud of.

And in talking to advisers with good business cards, most are only too keen to get out on the networking circuit to show them off.

Give and Receive Business Cards with Respect

Several years ago, I was speaking at the Asia Pacific Financial Planning Conference in Singapore. The great and the good from the profession in Australia, New Zealand, Singapore, Malaysia and India were in attendance and it was exciting for me to learn about the developments in the world of financial planning in those countries.

After my talk, many advisers came up to me and presented their business cards to me. I noticed a few things that I hadn't been expecting:

- They referred to their business cards as 'name cards'

- They bowed their heads slightly as they gave me their card

- They gave me their card using two hands

- They received my own card with two hands and spent an unusually long time touching, feeling and reading it.

With regards to the last point, whilst it is a cultural point to give and receive business cards with two hands, I observed how different it made the interaction between businesspeople. The simple act of using two hands to give and receive added an extra dimension of respect to the proceedings.

A financial adviser who spent many years working in the Asia Pacific region also told me that some people of 'higher status' will momentarily hold on to their card before letting go, as if to emphasis its importance and value.

Ever since then I have given and received business cards with two hands, and I urge financial advisers to do the same. Using two hands to give your card shows that your card is not something of low value to just casually hand over. You will feel a little awkward the first couple of times that you do it, but you soon get the hang of it and it is well worth the extra effort in how you present yourself to another person.

The Secret Code Within

QR Codes

It's worth adding more on the use of QR codes, because just adding one to the back of your business card is just scratching the surface of how they can be used in your financial advice business.

And if you're not entirely sure what a QR code is, here's the Wikipedia definition: *QR code is the trademark for a type of matrix barcode first designed in 1994 for the automotive industry in Japan. A barcode is a machine-readable optical label that contains information about the item to which it is attached.*

So now you know. Whilst once they were used to order automotive parts, today they are used in a variety of different ways. They've turned out to be a marketer's dream.

Of course, they don't just have to be used on the backs of your business cards. For example, if you still purchase DVDs in a store, you will often notice that on the back of the box is a QR code.

You simply point the camera on your phone at the code and by magic you start seeing the trailer for the movie playing on your mobile device. It's a brilliant sales aid and can easily be applied to a financial advice business.

With many financial advisers now using video in some way shape or form in their business, here is an opportunity for you to leverage it. Here are some ideas:

- Get video testimonials from clients and link to them via a QR code on the back of your business card

- If you have high quality paper brochures that you give to clients as part of your marketing materials, include a QR code which links to client testimonial videos

- You could also link a QR code to a video of one of your seminars or a PowerPoint presentation

- If you advertise in magazines or local newspapers, include a QR code that links to a video message, blog or your podcast. People don't always want to go to your URL/website address, but QR codes are still different enough that people are intrigued enough to scan them

- Similarly, if you advertise publicly in your local community, use QR codes in your advertising. I've seen QR codes being used on bus stops, advertising hoardings, local sports club noticeboards and shop windows where the adviser has a high street presence

- Use QR codes as an alternative way to generate sign-ups for your email newsletter

- Create a jigsaw puzzle of a QR code as a fun client giveaway, perhaps at a seminar or in a Christmas or Birthday card. The puzzle has to be put together and can then be scanned to reveal a video message

- Create a QR code as a sticker that is stuck to the inside of your rear car window. Yes, we love an old school idea and car stickers are still great value!

- Create a QR code as a temporary tattoo! I've seen a couple of professional advisers show off their 'new tattoo' in photos on Facebook, and followers are naturally intrigued to scan them and see where they are taken

- Strike up a relationship with a local coffee shops and advertise with a QR code on the side of their takeaway cups

- Add QR codes to advertising boards when you sponsor local sports clubs

- Add QR codes as advertisements in programmes for local theatre productions

- Use QR codes to take people to more detailed information that would not easily fit into a printed advertisement or promotion

- Add QR codes to paper napkins at your seminars or networking events

- Put a large QR code on the back of tee shirts so that people scan them as you walk down the street

- Add a QR code to your business card which links to your podcast page or your most popular episode

- Add a QR code to tea and coffee mugs that you give to clients as gifts. And yes, I've seen QR codes added as a topping to cupcakes at an adviser's coffee morning!

- Add a QR code to the bottom right corner of every slide in a presentation that you are giving at a seminar or event

- Promote a QR code, which when scanned can start playing music via the Spotify app. I've seen several advisers in the United States use their love of music as a differentiator – for example a financial planner who has a niche of working with clients who have a mutual love of heavy rock and metal.

   He has a regularly updated playlist on Spotify, and when his QR code is scanned by a client, it automatically starts playing his list. This is pretty smart in my view because people who are not clients can also scan his code and see if they like any of his musical choices.

   You could also do the same thing with art, music, sport, wine, travel and so on.

- I've even seen QR codes being added to the bottom of flip flops so that they make an imprint on wet sand when the tide is out…

As you can see, the opportunities are endless, but QR codes work because of the intrigue and curiosity factor.

Intrigue often prompts action and that's why they are effective. Many of the best website designers say that the highest converting websites are those that encourage visitors to interact with a site early on – even something as simple as a 'Where did you hear about us?' feature. Simply by clicking on one of several readymade options, can be enough to encourage people to stay on a site longer.

The same goes for QR codes, because the intrigue factor is sufficient to encourage people to get out their camera and scan to see what's behind the code, thus physically interacting with your promotion - and hence they are more likely to read further.

How do you generate a QR code?

Just go to Google and type in QR generator or similar. It's pretty simple to get going.

Priceless Free Marketing

Referrals

Most financial advisers tell me that referrals are their main source of new business – with the service that they have offered being the best marketing tool in their armoury.

We talked about trust earlier, and if happy clients are satisfied enough that they are prepared to recommend you, then you are doing yourself and the wider profession a service.

But the simple fact is, that whilst most financial advisers are indeed attracting referrals, many are not attracting anything like as many as they would like.

The evidence for this is that since I first starting meeting financial advisers in 1979, the number one question I was always asked and still see in online forums for the profession today is *"What's the best way to generate leads?"*

The answer is of course to offer an amazing service so that your clients will do your marketing for you. But the fact is, this question comes up time and time again – hence I am hoping that this book will help in some small way.

The overwhelming majority of financial advisers do not have a referral strategy. Yes, they provide a great service to their clients, but they do not have a formal plan that is designed to proactively attract referrals – preferring to *hope* that the great service will in itself create referrals.

It does to some extent, but with a formal referral strategy, you can supercharge the enquiries that you'll receive.

The top referral coach in the world is Bill Cates, and he just happens to specialise in helping financial advisers. One of the key things that Bill teaches is that the referral and introduction process should be a *collaborative* event between adviser and client – in that you work together.

This suggests that after you have worked with a client, you do not just sit back and hope for the best that he or she will introduce you. Neither is it as simple as saying at the end of a meeting *"Who do you know who could benefit from my services?"* as many advisers have been taught over the years. It goes much deeper than that.

In short, you need to teach or train clients *how* to recommend you rather than rely or hoping that they will do it. Bill often recommends going through with your client what they might actually say to people in order to make them more confident and deliberate in their introductory discussions. Examples of this are:

"What do you think you need to say to George that would encourage him to take my call?" or *"What do you need to say to Sue that could stir some interest in hearing from me?"*

You can see that questions like this will make the introduction to you far more intentional and personalised rather than the typical *"Oh, you ought to talk to my financial planner John Jones – he's great"*.

Bill also suggests encouraging the client to anticipate and be ready for any objections, by asking *"How do you think that George will react when you talk to him?"*. Again, this makes your client far more deliberate, careful and personal in their approach, thus increasing the likelihood that the referral won't fall on deaf ears.

Bill also advocates including a time frame so that you the adviser can justifiably get back to the client to thank them again and to enquire how they got on when talking to the introduction. In this way, they would expect you to follow up with them to enquire as to how the conversation went. Remember that your client has already experienced your great service and has already agreed to recommend you, so none of this will come as a surprise to them or make them feel awkward.

To many financial advisers, you personally might find this approach a little uncomfortable at first, but that's only because you are not yet used to doing it. But the more you role play this with colleagues, the easier it will become – indeed it will soon feel like a natural and professional thing to do with satisfied clients. In fact, you will soon question why you would *not* adopt this professional approach to building a referral strategy within your business.

Bill goes beyond this and advocates adopting a robust referral mindset, and I highly recommend his book *Get More Referrals Now! The Four Cornerstones That Turn Business Relationships into Gold.*

All financial advisers get referrals, but very few have been taught how to get more and better introductions. With a robust referral mindset and strategy, you can genuinely get to a point where you have a proven marketing strategy that has zero cost to your business, and which means that you need no other marketing activity within your business!

Wouldn't that be a great place to be?!

Check out Bill's book at https://amzn.to/2FaGixu

Going Round in Circles

Sponsoring Roundabouts

Now we're stepping into more old school territory. In fact, territory is the name of the game here. When it comes to sponsoring a roundabout, you have two options.

Firstly, it can be as simple as having a sign on a busy roundabout that says 'Sponsored by Jones & Co Independent Financial Advisers' – possibly including your phone number or website address.

Or secondly, you have a sponsorship arrangement where you work with the local council concerned to assist with the roundabout's maintenance and care – but with the focus on the environmental aspect by making it look attractive, plant flowers, trees etc. and attract wildlife. Whilst this is great news for the local area, it is of course valuable PR which will bear fruit over time.

What are the advantages of sponsoring a roundabout in your area?

- You differentiate yourself from your competitors

- Very high footfall or eyeballs on your advertising board

- Many people will see your advertisement several times a day – repeated exposure is important for success with advertising

- You become the only advertiser in that location, whereas local newspapers may carry multiple advertisements for competitors

- Unlike radio advertising, your advertisement can't be muted or turned over – it's difficult to ignore!

- Newspaper advertising typically has a shelf life of one day – most roundabout opportunities are 24/7 for up to twelve months

- Newspaper audiences are falling, whilst traffic levels are increasing

So if you are a financial adviser firm that wants to attract local clients, then roundabout advertising or sponsorship could be a great idea for you, particularly when combined with other forms of local promotion.

It certainly was for financial planner Keith Churchouse of Chapters Financial in Guildford who combined roundabout advertising with local radio appearances and said:

"We sponsored roundabouts for many years, which made a huge difference. Clients would hear me on the radio, see the name on a roundabout, then get in touch."

If you've got it, flaunt it

PR

When I first went self-employed, I met up with Jacqui – an experienced and highly respected journalist friend of mine who used to be a news anchor on BBC, ITV and Sky News. She asked me how I planned to promote myself and get my message 'out there'.

Social Media was just starting to kick off properly and that had got my attention, but I was also planning to run some seminars. Hopefully if I did a good job for clients, I might even get some referrals too.

But Jacqui asked me if I had got any PR planned, and to be honest I hadn't. I had always felt that PR was just for large organisations, and as far as I could see, it was a bit of a 'dark art'. I assumed that she meant sending out Press Releases, and whilst she pointed that there was a bit more to it than that, sending news to journalists was a good idea.

It also occurred to me that I didn't (yet) have any actual news to send out. But that was the point Jacqui was getting at – all of us have *more* news to tell people than we might realise. I'll explain in a moment.

Shortly afterwards I worked with Jacqui on a communication skills project with a firm of financial advisers, and whilst speaking to the group she started talking about the importance of PR. As a respected TV journalist, I figured she knew what she was talking about, and at the core of her message was that if you do anything in your business that might even be remotely newsworthy, you should tell the press – starting with local press and progressing to national and specialised press.

If you have moved offices, tell the press. If you have sent your staff on a training programme to improve their customer service skills, tell the press. If you have taken on a new software system to run your back office, tell the press. If you have sponsored the local kids' football team, tell the press. If you have hosted – or are about to host a series of seminars – you guessed it – tell the press.

In other words, whatever you are doing in your business, however trivial you might think it is – tell the press.

Jacqui went on to say that the vast majority of the content that you send to the press won't actually see the light of day and make it into the local newspaper or publication that you are contacting, so the inevitable question was asked by one IFA in the room...

"So what's the point?"

The point of course, is that by sending *regular* content to your local press – or the industry press for your target market, you are building a relationship with them. So that when the time comes that they want expert comment on a particular point, who do you think they will call?

You – or the financial adviser firm with whom they have a relationship.

Here in the UK we still have a vibrant consumer-facing press which publishes a huge amount of content relating to personal finance. In almost every article, there is learned comment from an expert, and often it is a financial planner. But you'll probably have noticed that the Press tend to ask for comment from the same small group of financial advisers every time. Why? Because they have a relationship with them and can be relied upon, so they don't even consider asking other advisers for their opinions. This happens at both a national and local level.

Take for example the topic of Brexit – however it pans out over the coming years, there will inevitably be questions that will come up on its impact on personal finances, investments, interest rates and so on. So who will journalists turn to for comments? Financial advisers who they know and like.

It's also worth mentioning that whilst much of the news that you send to local journalists does not end up in the printed version of the publication, it will often end up in the online version – thus helping you to be found by Google, Bing and other search engines.

It's also important to send news to your industry press for the same reason; build relationships – get known and get your comments appearing in the online versions of their publications so that you start appearing in search results for relevant enquiries.

Try this exercise:

Think back over the last six months and write down everything that has happened in your business that could even be remotely classed as newsworthy.

See if you can come up with six items:

1

2

3

4

5

6

When I do this exercise with financial advisers at live workshops, almost everyone can come up with six things that have happened over the previous six months – be it advisers in the firm have passed an exam, new clients came on board, the firm won an award or maybe they had started sponsoring a local roundabout.

If you can come up with one thing each month of the year, then you've got yourself twelve press releases, which will go a long way to building relationships with your local and national press.

Bonus PR Tip

If you are putting on local seminars, don't forget to invite local journalists to come along, and if they can't attend, send them a press release before and after the event.

Also, take the trouble to find your local newspaper journalist on social media, and occasionally tag them when you are posting content.

Walk on the Wild Side

Client Walks

I've heard of several financial advisers in the United States using client walks as a novel but valuable marketing initiative. If you send out regular press releases as highlighted in the previous chapter, client walks are just the sort of news that you can tell local journalists about.

And talk about an inexpensive marketing activity - not only does it cost you nothing, but it's great for your health and wellbeing too!

How does it work?

This is so simple, it doesn't really need much explanation. Inviting your clients to go on a walk is clearly a very social initiative and can be done throughout the year. Not only do you get to spend some quality time with them, but they also have the benefit of meeting each other and thus increasing their social circle. You are in essence, creating a walking community around your brand.

One of the reasons many people enjoy and stick to walking routines is because of the people they walk with, with some making new friends along the way.

The idea is not that you hope that whilst strolling through a leafy glade, the conversation will suddenly turn to investing and personal finance – it might do, but that's probably the last thing people want to talk about when they are out in the countryside. This is intended to be purely a social event that has real social, physical and mental health benefits for everyone.

Your walk can be as long or as short as you wish and doesn't necessarily have to be in the countryside. A city walk can be just as much fun.

All you have to do is:

- Promote your walk to your existing clients
- Pick a date, time, route and starting point
- Turn up and walk!

To put more flesh on the bones, I would suggest that after an initial trial, you make this a regular event, probably monthly. You could call it the *Jones & Co Walking Club,* or the *Smith & Co Financial Planning Ramblers* and you promote it through your email newsletter, on your website and your social media. You could take photos and video and use them in future communications and you should promote your walking club through a dedicated page on your site.

If your event is (say) the first Wednesday of every month, you could give your walk its own hashtag which can be used in social media posts – perhaps something like #WalkingWednesdays.

I know of one financial planning firm in the U.S. that creates a podcast recording along the way, where they interview clients while they are strolling through the countryside.

Your walk could be weekdays or weekends – it's up to you but will probably be determined by the type of clients you have and the amount of time they have available.

How long should the walk be?

That's up to you – but be guided by your clients. It could be anything from thirty minutes to four hours – you decide.

If you wish, you could take refreshments for a stopping off point, or maybe end up at a pub or coffee shop. The permutations on the theme are endless.

If you wanted to get creative, you could give each walk a theme or a challenge – perhaps with clues that have to be picked up and solved along the way.

Naturally, over time you will want to encourage attendees to invite a friend to come along. It may well be that your walkers will tell their friends anyway and that could lead to new referrals.

Walk and Learn

Another option is to foster relationships with local businesses by starting a walk at an athletic or outdoor footwear store. Before the walk begins, you or the store owner give a ten to fifteen-minute talk on selecting the right shoes or the latest outdoor gear.

It doesn't have to be an outdoor store – a local restaurant owner or their chef could give a short talk on how they source and work with local ingredients.

Alternatively, you could invite a local business owner to join you on the walk and you turn it into a low-key learning opportunity.

The point about hosting walks is that whilst differentiating yourself from other financial advice firms, you are also proactively adding value to your clients through something that is simple, inexpensive and potentially hugely enjoyable. When you first meet with new clients, it's a great thing to tell them about, with many wanting to be added to your walking mailing list there and then.

One final point – it's probably a good idea to check your public liability insurance as to the degree that taking clients on a stroll is covered. Just like a school will do before a trip, it would make sense to do a risk assessment in advance. Better to be safe than sorry…

Great minds drink alike

Wine Club

For those of you who feel that a less energetic client activity is in order, then consider hosting your own wine club or regular tastings. As with client walks, the point of this is to differentiate yourself by adding value to clients whilst enhancing the sense of community around your brand.

Most people like the occasional decent glass of wine, so here's a great opportunity to do something with clients that will be fun and a learning experience in a friendly and convivial environment.

If you are fortunate enough to have a vineyard in your area, then even better. If you are reading this book in the UK, you might be surprised to know that we have around eight hundred vineyards, so there's a good chance you will be able to find an expert to help you and local produce to try and buy. Take a look at www.englishwine.com/vineyards.htm

Now, there are wine clubs and there are wine clubs. Some are full or part time businesses that require careful planning and organisation – whilst others are very informal affairs. But for most financial advisers who are using this as a differentiation tool that also adds value to clients, you want to keep it simple.

It is far better and easier to approach a local vineyard or expert with a view to working with them. Some vineyards or independent wine traders will be more than happy to supply wines for your events and tastings, because obviously they are hoping to make some sales. Others will want you to make some purchases yourself.

Take a leaf out of Taurus Wines' book – an award-winning independent wine and drinks merchant in Bramley, Surrey. This is one of my personal favourite wine merchants who offer monthly tastings and educational events.

In their own words:

Taurus Wines - Wine School 2019

Join us at the shop on the last Friday of every month in 2019 for a series of informal, but informative wine education classes! Each session will focus on a key topic and the practical aspects of enjoying wine - perfect for budding enthusiasts or seasoned oenophiles alike.

Come along to one class or sign-up for a range: by the end you'll be able to identify the main wine styles, understand the principles of matching food and wine, and be confident choosing a bottle in a shop or restaurant. The classes would also make the ideal gift for someone who wants to know more about wine - vouchers can be packaged in a presentation box to make your gift that extra bit special.

All classes run from 7pm to 9pm on the last Friday of every month at Taurus Wines shop. All course materials, wine samples, water and water biscuits are included in the price.

January 25th

Wine Tasting 101 - Taste like a professional

February 22nd

Effervescence - Fizz, bubbles and everything that sparkles

March 29th

ABC: Anything But Chardonnay - The Marmite of the wine world

April 26th

Bordeaux: near and far - So uncool, it's cool

May 31st

Does red wine go with fish? - The principles of food and wine matching

June 28th

Old vs New - Worlds apart

July 26th

Rosé - Where there's a will, there's a rosé

August 30th

Off the beaten track - From Hungary to Lebanon

September 27th

Sweet at heart

October 25th

Age is but a number - The effect of time on a bottle

November 29th

Fortified wines - Not just for Christmas...

One class £35

Three classes £100

A year of classes £350

There is no reason why any financial advice firm can't model this approach or put on something similar, because ultimately it is a win, win, win situation for wine merchant or vineyard, financial advice firm and clients alike.

As to whether you absorb the cost yourself or make it a chargeable club for clients is up to you, but as you may know, I'm a big believer in using marketing techniques that can also become income streams in their own right – seminars being a great example.

Again, when meeting new clients you highlight your club as an added-value part of your proposition, and you promote it through your normal email newsletter, social media and dedicated website page. And don't forget to keep the local press updated and invite them along from time to time.

Whilst this is intended to be a vehicle to add value to your clients, clearly it is a differentiator for your business and one that you hope clients will want to share with their friends and colleagues. At each of your monthly events, you should make a point of encouraging client attendees to invite friends along next time.

Par for the Course

Golf Clinics and Other Niche Interests

Another permutation on the theme of leveraging clients' niche interests is to host your own Golf Clinic – or for that matter tennis, bowls, fishing or other sports and activities.

A while ago I heard about one IFA firm in East Anglia that has its own bridge club. The owner of the business has been playing bridge at a high standard for many years and after playing the occasional game with a couple of clients, he decided to broaden out his interest to his local community. Yes, he started with a press release…

It turned out that he had several other clients who played the game, and after just three months of running his club, he had attracted twelve further high-quality clients to his financial advice business.

Quite apart from the sense of community that hosting such events fosters, when people join special interest clubs – whether it's wine, golf, bridge or something else, one of the main benefits to them is the sense of making progress. Even if you are already accomplished at a particular activity, there is always scope for improvement and joining such a club will be very appealing.

When I first mentioned this idea at a workshop I was running for financial advisers, one asked me why someone would join any group that is run by a financial adviser! In fact, it doesn't matter who runs it, as long as people feel a sense of community, enjoy themselves and feel that they are making progress in their chosen activity.

According to one set of research, with the exception of younger professional bridge players, most amateurs are over the age of sixty, with many in their seventies and eighties – a prime market for many financial planners.

If that age group isn't your target market, then focus on another activity – perhaps golf. If you are a low handicap golfer yourself, then tell your clients that you're planning a practice session at your club or driving range and invite people along.

Or approach your local professional and pay for his or her time to run a clinic for you and your clients.

You don't need to have fifty people to come along to feel that this has been useful. Even if three or four join you, that is great because it will be valuable to them.

As before, when new clients come into your business, make a point of telling them that if they are a golfer, they are welcome at your regular golf events.

Golf is a good example because of the social aspect. Many financial advisers who are members of a golf club, inevitably attract more clients through word of mouth. Think how pleased they will be when they come to you for financial planning but discover that you also offer golf lessons!

This is one of the tenets of niche marketing – people are naturally attracted to others (including product and service providers) where they have something in common.

Which is as good a moment as ever to talk about fishing. To be specific, bass fishing…

Question – how many clients do you have who enjoy fishing for bass? One? Two? Any at all?

But I'll bet that if *you* enjoy bass fishing, you may well have a few clients who also do it.

And what if you publicised to the bass fishing community that a) bass fishing is your passion and b) that you specialise in financial planning for bass fishermen? How likely would it be that over time you would attract more and more clients who enjoyed the sport – either professionally or as an amateur?

Most financial advisers agree that dominating a niche market makes you much easier to be found within that market, and less of a needle in a haystack – but when I ask financial advisers what their niche is, they often find it difficult to identify.

When I started out as a Broker Consultant, I used to ask advisers on my patch this question all of the time because the answer would tell me whether or not they had the potential to be good and regular suppliers of PHI business – and indeed whether we as a provider were likely to be able to underwrite their cases quickly. Back in the 1980s, more often than not they would say:

- Accountants
- Police
- Nurses
- Doctors
- Surgeons
- Lawyers

- Professional sports people
- Musicians

Today, when I ask financial advisers the same question, I rarely get such precise answers, with responses such as the following being popular:

- Small Business owners
- Retirees in their sixties
- People living in West London
- Millennials
- Senior executives nearing retirement

Niche marketing experts would argue that even my first list (Accountants, Police etc.) is not niche enough, with the second list (small business owners, retirees etc.) not being niche at all. They will argue that the more niche you can make your target market, the more opportunity you have to dominate that market. So the first list should ideally look more like this:

- Tax accountants in the City
- Police Constables
- Oncology Nurses
- Eye Surgeons
- Immigration Lawyers
- Professional tour Golfers
- Classical Harpists

You see the difference? So the benefits of going niche in your financial advice business are strong and varied:

- Differentiation
- Less competition

- You have specialist knowledge and expertise which means you can increase your fees
- Greater visibility
- Greater likelihood of referrals and word of mouth introductions
- Closer client relationships
- Greater loyalty
- Lower marketing costs

That's clearly a list not to be sniffed at.

Fish where the Fish are

A brilliant example of this is Jared Reynolds CFP® from Columbia, Missouri. Jared is a partner in Wilkerson & Reynolds, an advisory firm in Columbia who specialises in working with bass fishermen.

He started out working with just professional bass fishermen, and because Jared and his father were fishermen themselves, professionals felt comfortable asking for help with their personal finances – in particular investing their often-considerable prize purses.

Jared also arranges fishing and hunting trips, and so gets to spend hours or even days at a time in close proximity with small business owners to form relationships.

For any financial adviser, it is well worth listening to Michael Kitces' interview with Jared as it gives fantastic insights into the value of working in a niche and how it can be subsequently expanded into other similar markets. Check out the Financial Advisor Success podcast interview at www.kitces.com/blog/jared-reynolds-wilkerson-bass-fisherman-niche-passion-prospecting/

Michael Kitces often speaks about the crisis of differentiation in the financial advice community, and focusing on a niche goes a long way to making you stand out from the crowd and attracting more of the clients you most highly value.

Not another Recruiter!

If I had a pound for every time a financial adviser has told me that they are fed up with recruiters connecting with them on LinkedIn… Maybe you are one of them.

So it amused me to discover one adviser who has taken the bull by the horns and chosen recruiters as a small niche market.

He has created a separate one-page website that is specifically aimed at recruiters, so whenever he is contacted by one on LinkedIn, he sends a message along the lines of:

"Hi Mike…

Thanks for contacting me on LinkedIn, it is much appreciated. I see that you are recruiter and I'll keep that in mind for the future.

You may be interested to know that dozens of recruiters have downloaded our special guide 'Twenty-one Proven ways for Recruitment Professionals to Save Tax and Increase their Income".

It's free and packed with valuable tips that I know you will find useful. You should get your copy at our website at www.jonesandcofp.co.uk.

Thanks in advance…

Mike"

As a result, he is picking up four enquiries a month directly from recruiters. You will also notice from his message that he is offering a lead magnet, and we'll come on to how this works shortly.

It's all about them – not you

Client Appreciation Events

There are multiple permutations on the client appreciation events theme, but I want to highlight the simplest and arguably most effective version using two examples.

Unlike a client seminar (we cover this later), workshop, symposium or 'weekend bootcamp' which are specifically designed to attract clients or create income streams in their own right, appreciation events are really there to do what it says on the tin – say thank you and give a nod of appreciation to your clients – and yes introducers and other interested parties and advocates.

They are also incredibly effective at attracting new client enquiries afterwards.

In terms of what you put on for your clients, you can generally be guided by your budget; but the format of the event is much the same however much you spend or where you hold it.

The golden format is:

- Evening event – primarily cocktails, wine and drinks for about an hour
- Welcome and thank yous from the host, plus any company announcements – ten to twelve minutes
- Introduction to the speaker or entertainment – two minutes

- Guest speaker or entertainment for forty-five minutes (maximum)
- More drinks and nibbles
- Send them away with a gift or memento of the evening

I have been the guest speaker at several such events hosted by financial advice firms, and this is the format which seems to work best in terms of timing, value, interaction, engagement, value for you and your guests and overall feedback.

Make absolutely sure that you choose your speaker or entertainment with a great deal of care. It is critical that you, the organiser have actually seen them speak/entertain – and ideally in person, though good speakers/entertainers will usually have a showreel on YouTube. Never, ever book speakers for client events without doing your homework, because they must be a good fit for your guests.

A financial planning firm in Wimbledon hired me to speak at their recent client event because their clients were predominantly lawyers, accountants, entrepreneurs, *"City types"* and retired versions of the same, and they knew that a) these people are my market and b) the IFA concerned had seen me speak at another event a few weeks earlier.

He also gave me the instructions to *"…keep my speech relevant to the attendees with quality content, but also humorous and entertaining"*. No pressure then…

Another financial planning firm Serenity Financial Planning followed a similar approach, and here is a copy of the Press Release that they sent to their local press in Lincoln after the event.

- Local independent financial planner hosts exclusive client event
- Clive Thompson of Serenity Financial Planning hosts first exclusive client event at the Cathedral Centre, Lincoln
- Exciting news and developments within Serenity Financial Planning announced over Canapés and Prosecco
- Clive Thompson showcased how a new approach to financial planning is proving popular in Lincoln

26 September 2016 – Clive Thompson of Serenity Financial Planning, Lincoln, hosted an exclusive evening called *'Canapés by Lincoln Cathedral'* with his clients at The Cathedral Centre, Minster Yard, Lincoln on Thursday 22nd September.

Clive provided an update on some exciting developments within Serenity Financial Planning including becoming a Registered Life Planner through the Kinder Institute of Life Planning.

Clive explained how Financial Life Planning takes traditional financial planning to another level by focussing on our more deeply held values, beliefs and aspirations that influence what we do. Those plans and dreams we've put off that were they to be included in a financial plan would lead to a more fulfilling life.

Clive went on to explain why he had pursued becoming a Financial Life Planner describing his journey from a traditional product-focused financial adviser to one that forges long term relationships with his clients focussing on their whole life and not just their money.

Serenity Financial Planning is the largest Financial Life Planning firm in the UK coupling coaching with truly independent financial planning to help clients really figure out what they want out of life before helping them realise their dreams and aspirations.

Clive commented,

"This event was everything I'd hoped it would be and more. Not only were my clients able to learn more about Financial Life Planning and our business, they were able to meet several members of the Serenity Team for the first time including founder Tina Weeks. All in a beautiful location.

The feedback has been amazing and it's inspired me to make this an annual event"

Tina Weeks of Serenity Financial Planning said,

"I was thrilled and honoured to be part of Clive's special evening and to meet his clients. More than anything, it was so wonderful to see and feel how much love they have for him. It was beautiful to see."

For further information, please contact:

Clive Thompson

ENDS

Clive later said to me,

"Looking back, I learned so much from the first event that helped me when planning the second one.

I remember you saying the magic occurs after the talking when the wine flows and guests get to mix and mingle. I discovered in both events that some clients actually knew each other but neither knew they were working with Serenity.

I loved the "community" feel we'd created. Following your advice, I chose a quirky venue next to Lincoln Cathedral and a time of year when we could go outside to the 'secret garden' - a walled garden overlooked by the Cathedral.

Throw in a live musician (an acoustic guitarist) and we had a fabulous atmosphere. Loved doing it!"

Quite apart from anything else, such news makes great content for an adviser's website, reminds clients that you host events and helps your site to be picked up in Google search results.

From my point of view, it is always an honour to be trusted with an adviser's clients for forty-five minutes, but what is always most noticeable is what Clive described earlier. Although most of the attendees have never met each other, magic happens when they do because they have something in common, and this can only be good for the perception of your financial advice firm.

As I mentioned earlier, this is just one format for client appreciation events, but the one that seems to be most effective. That said, I've also attended some very good 'annual client barbecues' outdoors in the Summer which start around midday with clients arriving any time between then and 2pm.

Again the focus is on food, drink and chat – often accompanied by a live musician in the background.

Whatever option you choose, don't forget to send out a press release afterwards like Clive at Serenity and also try to get some high quality (ideally professional) photos which can be sent to attendees afterwards and also put on your website. And while you are about it, get some video footage too.

Don't forget too, to tell people about your event in your client newsletter. Take a look below at what financial planners Jones Hill said about their client appreciation event:

Another year has passed, and we are proud to say another summer party has been successfully held for 2019. This is the third summer party we have held and it's safe to say it is the absolute highlight of our year and one which we all look forward to in the calendar.

We believe passionately in holding our client appreciation events each year as the cherry on the top of our client experience. This is not only to pay tribute to our honoured and respected clients who we like to call 'friends', but to also celebrate the successes we have seen them achieve this year and the years gone before. It is our privilege that we get to help clients achieve their dreams and see them become a reality!

As a small independent entity we believe in supporting other local businesses in the community, for that reason we chose to hold our event at The Glove Factory in Holt having previously held it at Hartley Farm, another beautiful location. Lots of preparation went into the event from co-ordinating catering, decorating, gifting and of course our superbly famous Ceilidh band.

The weather was a tad gloomy, but as the welcome glasses were being laid out, we were not going to let that dampen our spirits! Brian had taken a hop skip and a jump back from the lakes of Italy, joined by his lovely wife and Managing Director of the company Lisa. The scene was set for a wonderful evening...

As guests started arriving it was a delight to see whole families including children. Over the years we often get to know extended families by name and it's always a pleasure to get to meet them in person. Bobby and Jess also revelled in the opportunity to get to know clients they had not had the opportunity of meeting before.

Once everyone has been ticked off the welcome list and name badges handed out, everyone assembled for Brian's annual speech. As always Brian thanked everyone for coming and explained how super it was to not only see so many attend, but to also welcome new faces to the crowd.

On a final note everyone was reminded that there was to be strictly no 'financial talk' (or Brexit!) for the evening, that it was a very relaxed affair and encouraged everyone to mingle. These gatherings are always simply about having an enjoyable time with like-minded individuals.

Before we knew it, the band had started up and the first dancers were ready to show their moves! Everyone was clapping along, and others were twirling around. Many also got to experience the delights of our Magician, Damien, doing the rounds at people's tables. He was brilliant and at one point he had encased a card we had signed in a block of ice….as to how…. we still have no idea?!

Food was served and everyone enjoyed the delicious spread Kate, Ed and their team had put on for us. They had been superb in catering for a range of dietary requirements, also, there was plenty for everyone and the mini desserts were a real treat for all. Following this we had our annual group photo and thank you to my husband Ollie, who many of you will have spoken with, for just about managing to squeeze everyone in!

The final dance of the evening rolled around and there was hardly anyone left in their seats including those who had professed to 'not being a dancer' also getting involved and having a brilliant time.

As the evening drew to a close and we said goodbye to the final party animals (you know who you are!) everyone left with a gift bag in hand complete with locally produced

Bradford on Avon fudge by Megs Cottage which we hope you enjoyed.

We are already looking forward to next year's event and cannot wait to see you all again, with your dancing shoes at the ready!

Jenny and the Team x

PS: A special thank you to those of you who sent messages and wrote lovely cards of appreciation, all of which are shared with the entire team.

It sounds like a great event – and note the comments about it being "the cherry on top of the client experience".

As well as including a write up in your newsletter, post this as a blog on your website too, as this in itself could attract new clients.

In summary, client appreciation events are not just to say thank you, but to also add value and to help people feel part of your community. Financial Planning by definition may be an activity that looks to the future, but there are activities you can do in the here and now which help to cement relationships, build trust and encourage referrals.

Out of Sight, out of Mind

Out of Office Emails

For many years I have run online communities for financial advisers. They use the groups to network, share best practice, exchange ideas and to provide help and support to one another.

The majority of advisers share their email address with us when they join one of our groups, so we have a very large database of financial advisers to whom we send occasional email updates and news.

We have been sending our own email newsletter to IFAs and financial advisers since we started our first group in 2004, and it's proven to be a valuable way to reach our target audience. But what has been consistently fascinating to us, is the fact that whenever we send out an email 'blast', a certain percentage are returned to us because the recipient is out of the office. Clearly the percentage is quite high at certain times of the year such as holidays

Out of every one hundred Out of Office replies that we receive from financial advisers, almost all apologise for being unavailable, with about 50% suggesting that the recipient telephones the office to speak to someone else. Amazingly, an incredibly high number of Out of Office responses say little more than:

"We are out of the office and unable to respond. We will contact you on our return."

Literally, that is all that they say, and I can only imagine that this reflects very poorly on them in the eyes of the recipient.

To give those advice firms the benefit of the doubt, it may be that they are not aware that it is possible to customise the message…

However, even more startling, is that out of every 100 Out of Office messages that we receive, we estimate that approximately 97% fail to suggest that in the absence of the adviser, the sender could or should visit the company website.

It is bad enough that a great many Out of Office emails don't suggest calling an out of hours phone number, but that in this day and age, the fact that hardly any suggest to the recipient that they visit their website is somewhat alarming.

Here is a selection of places that you could direct people to via your Out of Office email:

- Your website
- Your latest blog post
- Your latest press and news page
- Dedicated individual pages on your site for investment information, pensions information, mortgage news, life planning service etc.
- Information about your forthcoming seminars or workshops
- A place for people to sign up to your email newsletter
- Your podcast
- Your YouTube channel

- Your online course
- Your free eBook or download
- Your book or publication on Amazon

To me, the fact that quite so many advisers do not include their website in their Out of Office message, suggests that many financial advice firms still don't take their website seriously as a means of communicating with clients.

And to be clear, this isn't necessarily about trying to attract new investment funds from existing clients – it's more about **adding value** and showing that you are a modern financial advice firm that cares about helping clients – even when you are not in the office.

And the side benefit that could result from this…? More referrals.

A Round of Applause

Congratulate local Movers and Shakers

One of the most popular features on LinkedIn, is the ability to send a quick message of congratulations to people when they have changed job or been promoted within their company. You have probably seen it in your notifications feed.

In fact, most people simply click on the ready-made Send Congratulations button, but at the end of the day, they still sent a message, and it is usually well received – often prompting a conversation between recipient and sender.

Why is this feature there? Because it encourages engagement between people – even when they are lazy and don't customise the message of congratulations. It is nothing more than a high-tech version of something we all used to do all of the time, here in the 'real' world.

As this book makes great pains to point out, for the most part financial advisers find it very difficult to differentiate from one another; at least from a consumer's point of view it is not easy to see at first glance how one advice firm is different from another. So doing something simple like saying congratulations to a local businessperson, fund raiser or community champion really will differentiate you.

And they are not hard to find. Get hold of your local newspaper, magazine or village magazine and at any given moment in time you'll find people who have been mentioned in your local press.

It might be your local butcher who has received an award in a national competition, or an accountant who has received recognition in their annual industry awards, or perhaps a local beauty spa who was highly commended in the local business awards. Wherever you are located, there will usually be someone to whom you could send a message of congratulations. In fact, these three examples were all in my own local newspaper over the last month.

How should you send your message? Either a letter, greetings card or postcard – usually much more impactful than an email. What's more, when sending it in a letter you should hand write the envelope so that it stands out from their other mail.

How about something like this:

"Dear Sue…

I spotted you in the local newspaper and just wanted to congratulate you on your recognition in the local business awards – you must be very proud.

All the best for the future and it would be great to catch up at some point to learn more about what you do. Let me know if I can introduce you to anyone.

Congratulations once again…

All the best

John Jones
Jones & Co Financial Planning

john@jonesandcofp.com"

There; how hard was that?

Note that there was no offer of a free financial review or similar – the idea is that this is a genuine attempt to wish someone well. You are doing little more than sending good wishes and potentially starting a relationship, which in time may bear fruit.

With a fair wind, your recipient will actually write back or give you a call to thank you for your kind message. It may sound contradictory in a book about marketing, but the name of the game here is to give without any expectation of anything in return, but a reply is all the opportunity you need to start a conversation…

"The name's Bond…"

Movie Afternoons

L et's step back into old school marketing territory once again and give our business a human touch.

If you are a family financial advice business (and there are many of them), a great tip is to host monthly or quarterly movie afternoons for clients who have young children or grandchildren. In fact, even if you aren't a family firm it's still something that any business can put on.

The idea is pretty simple – you go to the cinema! No business talk, no personal finance - just purely fun. Again, how hard is that to do?

It's entirely up to you as to whether or not you pay for the tickets, but even if you paid for (say) five families coming along, it's not exactly a marketing initiative that's going to break the bank. The key thing is to flag up your Movie Afternoons as something your firm does when you first meet new clients, highlighting that it's a fun thing that you like to do with clients who have children, grandchildren, nephews and nieces. In short, it falls within the added value part of your overall proposition.

You can have a special place to highlight your Movie Afternoons on your website and it's also something to include in your client newsletter, blog or other communications. With permission from attendees you can also include photos of everyone, complete with popcorn.

I know one adviser firm who takes between three and ten families to the movies once a quarter. He pays for the cinema tickets and then they all go for burgers afterwards, where everyone pays their share. Lots of photos are taken and everyone has a great time. At Christmas, instead of going to the movies, they arrange to go to a local pantomime.

You should already be able to see what a great differentiator this can be – how many other local financial advice firms do you know who do something as fun as this?

To my way of thinking, this is taking a local financial advice firm into something much more than a business that plans your financials. They are putting themselves at the heart of the local community and positioning themselves as fun, welcoming and family friendly.

And just imagine how the conversations will go when clients who have experienced your warmth are referring others to you. Wouldn't you love to be a fly on the wall to hear what they say…?

It's clearly not going to be something for all of your clients, but just knowing that this is something you do will position and differentiate your business in their minds.

Questions, questions, questions

Quora

Much of marketing for financial advisers these days, is about proving to the outside world that you have expertise, are trustworthy, friendly and professional. That's one of the reasons why so many people tell you that you should be blogging, putting out videos, writing books and hosting podcasts.

Clearly, not all of that is for every financial adviser, but it's important that one way or another you are able to show people that you are an expert in what you do.

Quora is a social networking platform for asking and answering questions. It first appeared in 2010 and follows a format that was once a feature on LinkedIn, where users could ask questions on any topic (usually business related), which experts would then answer. Answers to questions could then be upvoted or downvoted depending on their helpfulness.

It is not the most popular of social networking platforms but at last count it was receiving three hundred million unique visitors each month, which adds a level of credibility about it. However, Quora is extremely valuable as a platform with which to establish and highlight your expertise in a given topic. And the way you do that is to answer people's questions.

As I write, there are literally thousands of questions about personal finance. Many are very simple, whilst others require real expertise to answer. A sample of the questions currently on the site include:

- What are the most important things to know about personal finance?
- How do I improve my personal finances?
- What personal finance mistakes should everyone avoid?
- What is the most poorly understood area of personal finance?
- Why isn't personal finance taught adequately in schools?
- What are the best books on personal finance?
- What are the best personal finance tips for a twenty-four-year-old?
- How do I become a financial adviser?
- What is the difference between a financial adviser and a financial planner?
- What fees could I expect to pay for personalised financial advice?
- What is the single most valuable piece of financial advice you have ever received?

These are a sample of top-level questions, and there are many more which explore more specific areas of personal finance such as pensions, investments and life assurance.

Clearly, by answering questions on personal finance, you are highlighting your knowledge, experience and expertise. It is unlikely that you will pick up any new clients directly from people asking the questions, but over time you will raise your profile, be noticed for your expertise and your website will be visited. You can also hook up your Twitter and Facebook accounts to your Quora profile, so people will be inclined to also check you out on social media.

Quora also gives you stats and it's not unusual for your answers to be viewed up to five thousand times per month. The more questions you answer, the more views you receive.

That's one way of using Quora. Another is to turn your answers into a blog or even a book. For the blog, simply copy and paste the question and your answer onto your usual blogging platform – it's really that easy. Or, if you don't want to copy your answers verbatim, use the questions that people ask as a prompt or to give you ideas for a blog or other social media content.

You could also turn each question and answer into a short video that you post on your website, YouTube, LinkedIn or wherever else you like to post video content. Your answers could also form the basis of a podcast episode.

Your answers to questions on Quora are also a great way to create a book. The last time I looked, I noticed that I have answered sixty-one questions about LinkedIn on Quora, which is easily enough to form the content of a book – with each question being a chapter in its own right.

I have literally copied and pasted each question along with my answer onto a Word document. I can now publish it myself as either a paperback or Kindle eBook on Amazon, or I could format it as a PDF eBook which I give away as a lead magnet on a website.

Most financial advisers' websites are little more than a brochure. There is much that you can do to improve conversions from your website, but one of them is to highlight your expertise through sharing of your knowledge. Taking the content that you create on Quora in the form of answers to people's questions is a great way for people to get a sense of your expertise and value.

"He didn't rip us off"

Video Testimonials

As a conference speaker, I live or die on the testimonials I receive (or don't as the case may be). For most speakers, the single best way to attract more bookings is to give a GREAT speech or presentation, and there is a golden moment at the end of every presentation, where, if it has gone well, people will come up to you and say,

"Would you be able to give that exact same speech to my team next month?"

That golden moment is when audience members are (hopefully) feeling energised, inspired and eager to take action. But in the absence of people who are ready and able to book you there and then, a speaker still needs to take advantage of those few golden minutes, and the next best way to do that is to capture video testimonials.

Any speaker worth their salt always takes a microphone with them to conference bookings, which can be plugged into their mobile phone to capture a testimonial at a moment's notice. And it's not just speakers who capture video testimonials – increasingly businesspeople in a wide variety of industries and professions are doing so, because they are extremely powerful.

Testimonials caught during the golden moments are ideal – for example, many dentists now do this immediately after a patient has been in for teeth cleaning or whitening, the idea being to capture the patient's excitement minutes after treatment.

But videos don't always need to be caught within the golden moments – any video testimonial has its place, and they can be particularly effective for financial advisers.

One of my favourite financial advice firms for client testimonials is Jones Hill in Bradford on Avon in the UK. At the time of writing, they have a series of 'client stories' on their website featuring several different clients. Each one is extremely simple but very powerful, but what is most noticeable is how many of the clients featured talk about the human side of the relationship. This is a compilation video and well worth a watch:

http://bit.ly/JonesHillTestimonial

The videos are clearly professionally produced, but well worth the money. That said, they don't exactly need Steven Spielberg production levels, so the cost will be easily affordable by most advisers. Failing that, you could easily create your own client testimonial videos using your mobile phone.

If I was looking for a financial adviser in the Bradford on Avon area and I was comparing websites and financial planning services available, these videos alone would make the decision very easy for me. In fact, after seeing them I would probably not bother to look at any other adviser's website.

In addition to your website, make sure that you add your video testimonials to other areas of your online presence, including your LinkedIn profile, LinkedIn Company page, Twitter, Facebook, YouTube channel etc.

They could also be used as part of a client seminar or indeed to help promote any forthcoming seminars and events that you have planned.

It Can't be Unseen

Video Email and Messaging

O n the subject of video, it's also worth bearing in mind that video has its place as part of our day to day email communications. The marketing benefits of this are indirect, but it certainly adds to people's perception of us as individuals and plays very much the same role as the client testimonial videos mentioned earlier – i.e. they add a human and personal touch.

My favourite video email platform is BombBomb, who make the valid point that *"…video email highlights your greatest asset – you!"* In their own words:

"To be successful, you need to truly connect with your prospects and clients. But in today's inbox, basic email just doesn't cut it. BombBomb puts you back into your sales process and gets you face-to-face with the people who matter most."

BombBomb surveyed their users and the stats speak for themselves. The survey consisted of five questions – all asked in the same format.

"Compared to traditional, typed-out text emails, how much of a lift has simple video in email given you for the following:

- Generating replies and responses
- Getting clicks through your emails
- Converting your leads
- Staying in touch

- Generating referrals"

77% of people surveyed reported a lift using video in email with BombBomb.

20% of people doubled or more than doubled their results (reported a 100% lift or more than 100% lift) compared to traditional, typed-out text emails.

Overall results:

- 80.72% of people generate more replies and responses
- 87.03% get more clicks through their emails
- 68.21% convert more leads
- 90.10% stay in touch more effectively
- 55.88% generate more referrals

Other specific results:

- More than 1 in 4 people doubled or more than doubled their click-through rate with BombBomb video email

- More than 1 in 3 people doubled or more than doubled their ability to stay in touch

- Nearly 1 in 6 people doubled or more than doubled their replies and responses

- 1 in 10 people doubled or more than doubled their lead conversion rate and number of referrals with video email

So the benefits of video email are clear. Yes, it takes a little getting used to when you first start, but very quickly you become more and more confident.

To my thinking, in many ways this is a no-brainer. The modern financial adviser really needs to be using technology like this as part of their communication activities.

And if you are a LinkedIn user, the good news is that you can also send video messages through that platform. This is one of LinkedIn's 'hidden' features, and along with traditional text-based messages on the site, you can also send audio and video messages to people (via the mobile app).

Used with care, this is another excellent way for the modern financial adviser to differentiate him or herself.

The #1 Single Most Effective Strategy Ever

Seminars and Client Events

This is one of the big ones. In fact, I go so far as to say that seminars and workshops are probably the single most effective form of marketing that a financial adviser can do.

Yes, doing a great job with a client and getting a valuable referral is pretty powerful, but that only goes so far. Not only are seminars proven to attract high quality new clients, but they also add significantly to your overall proposition as a financial adviser. They can also create a valuable new income stream in their own right.

It is a fact that many of the most successful financial advisers around the world, use seminars and workshops at the heart of their business. And when an event is combined with social media, video and other communication technology, the overall impact of your event can be considerable.

Let's look at some of the benefits of financial advisers hosting their own events:

- Try before you buy - potential clients get to *see and experience* you, your product and your service in action, before they make a purchase.

- Just holding the event at all positions you as an expert on the subject concerned – if not *the* expert.

- 'Seminar Selling' as it is often called, is incredibly cost effective. Even if you don't charge a fee for attendance, consider your current cost of acquiring a client and compare it to the cost of having a room full of warm customers. The fact that they have turned up at all makes them a warm lead by definition, so you have multiple prospects all present at the same time.

- Seminar Selling is even more cost effective if you charge an entry fee. In fact, if you do, your delegates or attendees are paying to be your prospects! I am aware of many financial advisers who started out using seminars as a marketing tool, but who ended up earning more income from charging an entry fee to their events than from their traditional financial planning services.

- Hosting a seminar or workshop gives you the opportunity to promote additional products and services, thus making the event even more profitable.

- Speaking to a room full of people and *just demonstrating your expertise* actually takes the pressure off you, as you are not overtly trying to sell your product or service. I repeat, seminars are a demonstration of your expertise and the chance for people to see what you do 'live', so there is no need to make a blatant sales pitch for business.

- Seminars enable people to form a more detailed and valued opinion about you. This helps them to build trust without having to speak to you. They can also look at the reactions of other people in the audience and gauge how they too are responding.

- Conversion rates at seminars can be extremely high. By conversion rates, I mean people who approach you later with a view to purchasing your main product or service, or who approach you for a personal consultation based on your expertise.

  Andrew Brown, a financial adviser based in the South West of England wrote to me:

  "(Our) seminars would typically be attended between 35-55 people, and the conversion rate was always extremely high and often approaching 100%."

  Enough said…

- Referral rates can be incredibly high too, with an abnormally high percentage of attendees telling their friends and colleagues about you and your event afterwards.

- Of those attendees who do not subsequently approach you, you have at least warmed them up for another day. A key skill in Seminar Selling is relationship building, so that even if they are not ready to make a purchase now, they may wish to in the future.

- Holding a seminar or workshop can massively increase your list of contacts for your email newsletter or other communications. Regular communication with clients or potential clients is essential for any small business and a newsletter is an ideal way of doing this.

That said, do not discount the idea of also sending out a high-quality *paper* newsletter. Martin Bamford, a very tech-savvy financial adviser in Cranleigh, UK produces an excellent and high-quality paper version of his email newsletter, which is very well received by his clients. And if you produce a paper newsletter, it makes a great giveaway to attendees of your seminar or live events.

- Some people find that after holding a few seminars or workshops, new doors unexpectedly start to open for them. It is possible to get very well known in a particular field and consequently be in demand as an expert speaker on your subject.

  Some people even find their seminars are so successful that their presentation becomes more in demand than their main product or service. This also can lead to more speaking work, private consultations and consequently the need to completely re-engineer their business.

- Seminars and live marketing events are a great way to raise and enhance your profile locally. Martin Bamford who I mentioned a moment ago, told me that he has attracted new clients from people who did *not* attend his seminar because they couldn't make it, but just seeing the promotions for his event was enough to persuade them to make contact with him.

I could go on, but the long and short of it is that seminars and client events work on a number of different levels. The perceived downside to this is that they are difficult, time consuming and expensive to set up and put on – particularly if you have never run one before. These questions are very common amongst financial advisers:

"How many people should I invite?"

"What is the ideal number of attendees?"

"How much budget should I allocate to my seminar?"

"How long does the planning take?"

"What topics should I cover in my seminar?"

"What are the best days of the week to hold seminars – and is there an ideal time of day?

"How do I go about marketing and promoting my events?"

"Do I need to buy a list of potential attendees?"

"Won't people just come along for the 'free lunch'?"

"What if I don't get many bums on seats?"

"How do I follow up my events?"

"Should I invite guest speakers?"

"What if I'm not very confident speaking in public?"

The good news is that all of these questions have been asked many times before, and they all come down to a process. Follow the process to the letter and you won't have anything to worry about.

Marketing and promotion is one of the biggest worries. Time and time again IFAs and financial advisers tell me that they really want to put on some seminars or client events, but they hold off because they don't know how to get started. Follow the process and all your worries will be taken care of.

That exact process is outside the scope of this book, but if I have whetted your appetite, my book *Successful Seminar Selling for Financial Advisers* gives you chapter and verse on everything you need to know to plan, promote and present your own seminars. You can get your hands on it at https://amzn.to/2pO1FzG

Worksite marketing

Don't forget either, opportunities for worksite marketing. If you target businesses and the HR departments of local organisations, there will often be occasions when you can run a seminar or presentation directly to staff at the premises of your client company.

The exact same benefits apply as hosting public seminars, but the fact that you are in the building often implies to staff that you have been 'endorsed' by the business – thus increasing the likelihood that you will receive enquiries afterwards.

The general setup of the worksite marketing opportunity will vary by business that you are working with, but the concept is exactly the same. Your time slot will often be quite short (lunchtimes, tea breaks, night shifts etc.) and occasionally you will find yourself presenting in some unusual locations. I have presented in car showrooms, aircraft hangars, hay lofts on farms and wearing a hard hat in a heavy machinery plant – so have fun!

Client feedback events

Again, another permutation on the theme, and one that can make big changes for the better to your business.

Your format can be anything you wish – formal round a table or more relaxed over drinks and cocktails, the idea being to get a group of valued clients in the room and to get feedback on everything you do from your marketing to how quickly you answer the phone.

You can follow a set agenda or keep it conversational in style. Online or paper client surveys have a lot of value, but you can't beat face-to-face. The only downside is that some clients may not feel inclined to be as open or critical as they might otherwise be if they were answering an anonymous survey, so you will need to think carefully about the questions you ask. Look for specifics and detail on various aspects of your business wherever possible.

In many ways, client feedback events are the opposite of you running a seminar. Instead of you communicating value to the prospects/clients, they are communicating value to you.

Quite apart from the ability for you to get feedback on your marketing and services, simply getting people in a room will be another touchpoint and could be just the prompt they need to refer a friend to you. In fact, at the end of the feedback event you should make a point of saying how grateful you are as a business *"...when valued clients like you recommend us to others"*. And if you read Bill Cates' books on referral marketing, you will also learn how to teach clients to refer you.

In short, seminars, client events and worksite marketing opportunities are remarkably effective as a marketing tool. Yes, they take a bit of work, but follow the process and you will wish you had started this years ago.

Feed them, but leave them wanting more

Webinars

Webinars have traditionally had two roles in business:

- To promote and sell something
- To educate and add value

In fact, webinars are a perfect marketing medium for financial advisers and do a lot more than just education and promotion. Here are over twenty advantages for advisers:

1. Hosting webinars differentiates you from other advisers
2. Webinars are a great way to repackage your expertise into new formats
3. Webinars are a perfect way to highlight how you apply your expertise in the real world
4. Webinars are simple and easy to create, produce and broadcast
5. Webinars can deliver massive value to your target market
6. Hosting webinars develops authority and trust
7. Webinars enable you to communicate with multiple people simultaneously

8. Webinars can enhance business relationships with local professional connections
9. Interactive webinars help you to engage directly with your target audience
10. Webinars keep your audience engaged with you and your content
11. Holding webinars raises brand awareness
12. Hosting webinars are affordable and very low cost
13. Webinars can be re-purposed into other types of content
14. Webinars can be recorded and replayed multiple times
15. Webinars can be an additional revenue stream when you charge for attendance or viewing
16. Webinars build your list and generate qualified leads
17. Webinars generate referrals
18. Webinars are a great way to share news and views with clients on a regular basis – and an alternative to sending out an email newsletter
19. Webinars are a perfect way to promote and sell other services that you offer
20. You can feature guest speakers and presenters on your webinars
21. Webinars are a great way to follow up after your seminars and client events
22. Webinars are an ideal early step on your value ladder, leaving people wanting more

So why don't more financial advisers host them?! My research suggests three reasons:

- Advisers have often participated as audience members in a webinar, but have never had the benefits of hosting them explained to them

- They have concerns about the technical aspects (which platform, how to get started etc.)

- They are unsure about what content to feature in their webinar

In many ways, hosting a webinar is much the same as a traditional seminar. Or, think of it as an online version of your newsletter and choose content accordingly.

Yes, it's OK to host a one-off webinar but the real benefits are to be had when you host them on a regular basis. Once a month is great, but every quarter will be fine too. When you consider the depth of knowledge that financial advisers need to have, you can see that you will never be short of content to present. Best results will come when you plan your webinars in advance, giving you plenty of time to put it all together.

How long should your webinar be?

That's entirely up to you. I've run webinars lasting over four hours, but to be honest that is a bit excessive unless you are hosting something more like an online course or training session. Webinars for financial advisers can be anything from thirty minutes to an hour – so before you get started, put yourself in your audience's shoes and ask yourself what topics and timescales would work best for *them*.

As for the webinar platform that you use, there are plenty to choose from, but for most financial advisers

Zoom is as good a tool that you will find anywhere. Most advisers are already familiar with Zoom as a video communication platform that they use for online meetings with clients, and it has an add on feature that turns it into a webinar tool.

It includes a registration page, confirmation emails, the ability to brand your webinar broadcast with your logo, stats on who watched the webinar and also records it automatically so that you can use it again.

Being able to pre-record your webinar and play it as if it is going out live is also useful if you don't yet feel ready or confident to present it in real time. My advice is to put together a practice webinar, which you show to your colleagues first, so that you can hone it before doing it in front of clients.

If you are looking to use webinars as a promotional tool for seminars, online courses and digital products that you want to sell, there are some advanced techniques to structuring your presentation. If that is something of interest, please drop me a line and I can point you to some useful resources.

In summary, just like seminars and client events, webinars are another way of doing the same thing – but which have their own distinct benefits. What's more you don't have to worry about hiring a venue and getting in catering!

Webinars are also ridiculously easy to do, and given all the advantages above, advisers really should consider including them in their marketing and communications mix.

"Unaccustomed as I am…"

Public Speaking

If you have taken a liking to presenting at seminars, workshops, client events and webinars, then there's a fair chance that you will want to consider taking the next step with a move into more public speaking.

Many financial advisers are asked to speak at an event at some point during their career, but that is usually on a reactive basis. Consciously deciding to do more public speaking is a different matter altogether, but one which can have significant benefits for your business. Indeed, it is not uncommon for speaking to become a core part of your business model. Not only can public speaking be a powerful and proven marketing tool, it can be a highly profitable activity in its own right.

In consultancy sessions with financial advisers, 'moving away from the regulated environment' is a common goal I hear from many IFAs and speaking and training ticks this box nicely. Indeed, financial advisers in the USA picked up on this many years ago when many realised that much of their face-to-face financial planning business was unprofitable. Still passionate about helping clients to achieve their goals, but not wishing to retire from giving financial advice, many advisers decided to start hosting more seminars and to embark on the speaking circuit.

"But don't I need to have been a politician, written a book or won an Olympic Gold Medal to go on the speaking circuit?"

These things certainly help but are far from essential. What audiences want to hear is passion, expertise, a hint of 'edutainment', value and ideally a good story. In fact, when politicians and Olympic sportspeople go onto the speaking circuit, it is usually their story that got them there.

When I run presentation skills and public speaking training for financial advisers, the main thing we focus on is finding their story – and guess what, it turns out that everyone has a story to tell. The skill is teasing it out and recounting it in a way that makes others eager to hear more.

- Who I am
- Where I came from
- How I got to where I am today
- The obstacles I overcame along the way
- What I believe in
- My values
- Lessons I have learnt
- Mistakes I've made
- The lightbulb moment
- What I tell my kids

…are all things that people like to hear from any speaker, professional or otherwise – and most financial advisers have much to offer from this list.

Yes, writing a book is a big help if you want to do more public speaking, and financial planners in the USA have this very much higher up their priority list than UK advisers, though not just to support their public speaking. We'll cover this in a later chapter.

A good place for financial advisers to get into speaking is their local secondary school. Personal Finance is becoming more important in the school curriculum, with many bringing in guest speakers on a wide variety of topics. My wife is a school careers lead, and I know that she has brought in a local IFA to speak to students.

Don't expect to always be invited to speak on personal finance issues – schools are also interested in your take on the joys or otherwise of following a career in financial planning – or paraplanning for that matter.

Also, don't expect to get paid much, if anything for speaking in schools, though private schools often have decent budgets. There are also dedicated speaker bureaus and agents for school speakers which will help you to find opportunities.

Either way, if you can get the hang of speaking to anything between thirty and thirteen hundred teenagers, you can handle any audience from there on!

A quick tip – if you do get to speak in a school, always make sure that you have a handout covering your key points. Your handouts will often find their way home with many parents and carers taking a keen interest in them. In short, yes – speaking to school students can and often does lead to parents getting in touch wanting to discuss their own financial arrangements. Some may also invite you to come and present at their company or place of work.

Deciding to get into public speaking either for marketing purposes or the new income stream is a mindset more than anything else. It's not for everyone, but those who do take it up usually find it hugely rewarding for a variety of reasons.

If you are interested, I would highly recommend that you consider going along to your local Toastmasters group where you will learn about speaking technique etc. But my main recommendation would be to join the Professional Speaking Association (PSA in the UK) or the National Speakers Association (NSA in the USA) or your local country equivalent.

There you will learn about the art and business of speaking, how to market yourself as a speaker, how and when to charge fees and so much more. Members tend to be a fantastic mix of complete beginners and newbies, right through to world renowned motivational, inspirational and business speakers. I have introduced several financial advisers to the UK PSA, and they have all found it extremely valuable. One financial planner (Jason Butler) was even asked to speak to Fellows of the PSA at their annual conference.

Those of you reading this who are members of MDRT (Million Dollar Round Table) will know that the annual convention is one of the largest conferences in the world (from any industry) and features amazing speakers from within the financial advice community and wider industry and commerce. So if you are an adviser thinking that there might not be much call for personal finance or financial services speakers, you should think again. Everyone, whatever their industry, has a story to tell and lessons they can share.

If you would like to join the PSA in the UK, some membership levels may require someone to refer you, so if this is something you are considering, please let me know and I can refer you myself.

Their website is at https://www.thepsa.co.uk

In summary, public speaking is a proven and powerful way to market and promote yourself and your business, and which in turn can create a valuable new income stream in its own right. What's not to like...

Feed your Fish

Online Communities

Many financial advisers reading this book will have first heard about it in one of my online communities on LinkedIn or Facebook. Those groups would in turn point them to Amazon where they purchase the book.

In fact, I set up the world's first online community for financial advisers back in 2004. It started life as a group within the Ecademy.com social networking site, and as technology tastes changed, we created groups on LinkedIn, Facebook and elsewhere.

The current main group (LifeTalk) is on Facebook and is incredibly active with 80% of the membership engaging with the content each month. IFAs and advisers use the group to network, share best practice, exchange ideas and to provide help, guidance and support to one another. Many advisers have told me privately that the content in the group has often helped them to make major and extremely valuable business development decisions.

The truth of the matter is that whilst the groups are incredibly valuable for peer to peer networking, they are in fact marketing tools that I use to keep my prime target market (financial advisers) 'within my sights'.

Typically what most businesses do is to set up a website and then wait for their target market to visit it. They do this through a variety of methods which range from sitting back and hoping, through to much more proactive activity such as Facebook advertising etc.

But what many businesses forget, is that more often than not their target market congregates online in forums and Facebook and LinkedIn groups – just as they might go to an exhibition or business show that is relevant to them. So if I want to find large groups of financial advisers, I can go along to the Personal Finance Society conference and other events – but much cheaper and easier is to find them in online groups. Even better if I personally own the online group.

I liken having an online group to owning a fish tank, where the fish are your members. And if you have a tank full of fish, you need to keep them alive and thriving by feeding them on a regular basis.

On a Monday morning you need to feed your fish. By this I mean you need to add content that attracts the members in and which they consume.

On Tuesday you feed your fish again – adding more content which is of value to your target audience. In this case, financial advisers.

On Wednesday you do the same thing – feed them with more content that they will find useful in their day to day lives and businesses.

But what happens if you forget to feed them on Thursday? Guess what – they still turn up because they have come to associate your group with quality 'food' and value.

If you also forget to feed them on Friday, very often, many members will bring their own food which they will share amongst one another. And so it goes on, day after day.

That's the secret of building any online community – feed your fish, day after day.

In time, the amount of food that you the owner need to put in the tank decreases significantly, to the point where the members feed themselves and the community runs itself. But all the while, you, the owner are watching, observing and taking notes on:

- What topics they talk about
- What questions they ask each other
- What problems they have
- What issues they really care about
- Etc.

And the data you gather is amazing – giving you incredible and detailed insights into the key issues faced by members of your community. And when you know that, you can either create products and solutions that you know they will be interested in purchasing or you can attract advertisers and sponsors who already have answers to their problems.

So from my point of view, one of the main topics that come up time and time again in LifeTalk is Lead Generation. Whilst on the one hand advisers say that referrals are their main source of new client enquiries, the fact that questions about lead generation come up so often in the community, suggests that perhaps they do not yet have sufficient high quality referrals to go round, and that they need to explore additional ways to attract new prospects.

And that's why, including this one, I have written seven books on marketing and lead generation for financial advisers.

In short, my community tells me what products and services I need to create to serve their needs. And they tell me through the medium of my online groups on Facebook and LinkedIn.

Don't wait for prospects to find and come to you. Go to where they already congregate online or create a place of value for them to visit and hang out. Feed your fish and then give them bait to bite on. When you give them food that they *really* enjoy, they will more than likely bite down hard...

So how could this approach work for financial advisers?

There tend to be four ways that creating online communities can be of value to advisers:

1. Where you operate in a strict locale
2. Where you have a clearly defined target market or tight niche
3. Where you want to add value to existing clients
4. Special initiatives

Let's look at each in turn:

Location based communities

This is the easiest and most common. If you live in (say) Guildford in the UK and you only want to focus your attention on prospects in that area, you could create a Facebook group for people in that region. It is true that there are already multiple location-based Facebook groups, but there is always room for more, particularly if you give it a theme.

For the avoidance of doubt, you could join an existing location-based group and add value within the group (note 'add value') and this approach can work well, but ideally the group should be set up and run by you and your team.

Target market and niche groups

These types of groups are the most fun, because they revolve around a topic, specific client type or niche market.

Earlier I mentioned Jared Reynolds whose target market is people who fish for Bass. And ideally professional Bass fishermen. That's what I mean by niche.

But you don't need to go that deep into a niche. If you target Doctors, then you could create an online community for them. Equally if you target Lawyers, you could create a group for them with content that meets their needs.

Maybe you enjoy football and would like to serve others who follow the sport – again you could create a group which revolves around that topic, but which is run by and associated with your brand.

You might be surprised just how popular football is in online communities. Even on LinkedIn, you will find dozens of groups related to Manchester United.

In short, if you target a specific type of group or niche, create a group for them and the people will come.

Existing clients

Another approach is to create a group for the community you already serve – your clients. And for that matter, your professional introducers too.

Think of your group as an additional part of your value proposition and position it as such. Every time you meet a new client, tell them that you have an online private group for clients where they can meet others like themselves, ask questions and share content of their own.

They won't all join, but it will certainly add something extra to their relationship with you.

If you wish, you could restrict membership to a certain type of client. Many advisers segment their clients, and if that's something you do, you might want to consider offering membership of your group to your top tier of clients. It's up to you.

Another option is to charge a membership fee for your private group. Again, this isn't for every adviser but it's certainly something to consider if you are looking for new ways to differentiate yourself and to develop new income streams.

Special initiatives

A great way to use online groups is to create a community based around a special initiative or something that you create specifically to attract clients – i.e. a lead magnet.

Catherine Morgan is an award-winning financial planner and money coach at The Money Panel. In a relatively short period of time, Catherine has become very well known for her financial coaching work with women and has been featured in a number of high-profile newspapers and publications.

A key part of her proposition also doubles as a lead magnet, and which simultaneously builds community around her brand.

Many internet marketers use challenges as a way to attract clients, often fairly simple such as a 30-Day Challenge which helps you to form new habits in a fun, friendly and no pressure environment. Catherine uses this approach with her **Five-Day Free Challenges** which she promotes on her website and on Facebook. Typically the challenge will be money related, and in one example to:

- Help you identify what relationship you have with money
- Unlock self-limiting beliefs that are holding you back
- Give you 100% confidence and control with money
- Pay yourself first and plug financial leaks forever
- Create great financial foundations

Creating a group on Facebook (or anywhere else for that matter) can be a key part of such challenges where members can interact and engage with each other – asking questions and giving feedback on their progress. The community aspect is just as important as the outcomes from taking part in the challenge, but in the process, Catherine has got a captive audience with whom she can engage both during and after the event.

Some readers of this book will remember the Financial Adviser Mastermind and Challenge which I ran in 2019. This was a week-long initiative where I interviewed thirty industry experts on how to run a successful financial planning business. It was hugely popular and valuable for the advisers who watched it, but at the same time gave me an opportunity to engage with a large number of professionals in my target market through the medium of a support community online.

As financial advisers we are only limited by our own imaginations as to how we can use challenges and online communities to both attract new prospects and to add value to our existing clients.

Your community platform

I've already mentioned that there is a choice of platform where you can create your community or group. The cheapest and easiest are Facebook and LinkedIn groups. They are also very well-known and many of your target community members are already using these sites, so they will be familiar with how they are set out and work. And to some extent, many people are addicted to these two sites, so should be more than comfortable joining any group that you set up.

Whilst these are the main advantages, there are also disadvantages you need to think about, such as:

- They are owned by someone other than yourself. Both Facebook and LinkedIn could get rid of groups at a moment's notice.

- The content that your members see is controlled by their respective algorithms. So you can post content in your group and there is no guarantee that your members will actually see it.

- The algorithm also favours people who are regular visitors, so those members who get a lot of value from your groups but who don't visit particularly regularly, often miss out.

- Both Facebook and LinkedIn make money from advertising. Just as you currently see advertisements in your Facebook feed, it is all but inevitable that they will introduce advertising into the group news feed at some point.

- LinkedIn and Facebook are designed to be distracting, and that also includes distracting to members of your groups. Even when someone is browsing your group, they are seeing advertisements for other (possibly competitive) groups – not to mention the wealth of clickbait posted by others.

Yet despite these downsides, LinkedIn and Facebook groups are extremely popular, so what other alternatives are there?

For me, there is one community alternative which stands head and shoulders above anything else, and that is a platform called Mighty Networks. This is a 'software as a service' platform which enables you to create online communities accessible via your own app or laptop/desktop computer. The key benefits are:

- No algorithms telling people what to see
- No advertisements
- No distractions
- The ability to include niche sub-groups within your community
- The ability to add courses and trainings
- Polls
- Events
- Membership categories

On the downside, whilst Mighty Networks as a platform is extremely easy to navigate and get used to, people are still moderately obsessed by the more well-known platforms, so your content will need to be outstanding to encourage people to modify, if not change their habits.

Like all things, you pay your money and take your choice. Whatever platform you choose, building community around your brand is one of the very best ways to attract new people to your business and to build your referral mechanism.

I have been running online communities since 2004. If you would like to ask a question – perhaps about setting up your own, please don't hesitate to contact me at philip@financialadvice.marketing.

Bowled Over

Local Sponsorship and Community Involvement

Once again, we step into old school territory, but a marketing approach that also benefits from today's tech.

Put simply, local sponsorship can be an easy and inexpensive way to raise your profile locally, whilst also supporting your local community. Examples can include:

- Sponsoring shows and events at your local arts or community centre
- Sponsoring the shirts of a local football team
- Supporting a kids local football team
- Sponsoring your local tennis club
- Sponsoring show ring activities at your County Show
- Sponsored photo booths at local dances and events
- Sponsored live streaming or live tweeting of a local event
- Sponsored Free Wi-Fi at events
- Sponsored charging stations for mobile phones at events
- Sponsor local business awards
- Sponsored Welcome Drinks at local events
- Sponsored play areas for kids at a local event or sports centre
- Sponsorship of 'Digital Goody Bags' after a live local event – a brilliant way to get email addresses and to send people to your website
- Etc.

We are really only limited by our own imaginations when it comes to what we can sponsor locally. I've even seen the 'VIP Toilets' at a polo match being sponsored by a local business.

Whatever you decide to sponsor, always think about the social media opportunities that could come from them – what could we build into the sponsorship or activity that would encourage people to tweet or post on Instagram, Facebook – or even LinkedIn for that matter?

One of my favourite examples from a financial planning firm was also one of the most effective in terms of reaching their target market – and also one of the least expensive.

Jeremy Squibb of Serenity Financial Planning in Cornwall sponsored Porthleven Bowling Club. In addition to an advertising board around the bowling green itself, they also had their logo and text on the club's website.

Serenity Financial Planning is a national company but run locally by Jeremy Squibb who is a Helston man and has lived here all his life. Some of our members already use his services to manage their financial arrangements and would certainly recommend Serenity to everyone else. And here's the link to their web site etc…

What could be simpler?! And note the social proof included in the wording "Some of our members already use his services…"

Serenity's investment: £340 for five years. That's lust over £5 per month.

Jeremy went on to sponsor a trophy for the club which he presented, and where photos were taken for the website and local press. His investment: £150

The key thing is to get involved with local sponsorship where you know your target market is going to be present and where they will see your promotion. Jeremy is now adding sponsorship of a local Walking Football group for over-fifties who want to stay fit and healthy.

No Walking Football group in your local community? Set one up!

Getting involved with your local community potentially means that everyone wins. You actually get to help local initiatives, which is great – but it also makes your business highly visible. Take a look at Informed Choice Independent Financial Planning's 'Community' page on their website at https://icfp.co.uk/about/community for some ideas.

As well as the great work they do, having a page on their site dedicated to it helps with search engine visibility and positioning. It's also valuable as powerful local PR.

By Hook or by Book

Write a Book

Now, we combine old school marketing with the latest in technology. The more observant reader will have noticed that I have mentioned writing a book a couple of times so far, but until now not in very much detail.

In my view, the most effective of all marketing approaches for financial advisers are:

- Building a clear and robust referral strategy – get this right and the rest of this book becomes redundant.

- Host seminars, workshops and client events – proven time and time again to be ridiculously effective for financial advisers.

- Convert more of the people who already visit your website – financial advisers' conversion rates on their website are generally appallingly low.

  And…

- Write a book.

To many readers, writing a book will sound like a great deal of hard work and a step too far – particularly if you have never written anything longer than a tweet, blog post or article for your local paper.

So let's start by looking at why it might be a good idea – and for the avoidance of doubt we are talking about writing a non-fiction book:

- It differentiates you from other financial advisers – particularly when prospects are looking for local financial advisers

- It positions you as an expert on your topic (if not one of *the* experts)

- It is the best business card you will ever give away

- It is a high value early step on your value ladder

- It helps to develop or enhance your brand

- It opens doors that might previously not have opened for you

- It elevates your status amongst the financial advice community (good for PR which gets visibility in search engines)

- It elevates your status in your local community

- It helps to attract speaking engagements – some of which will pay high fees

- It positions you as a local expert in the eyes of local press, TV and radio

- It gives you an additional product to sell

- It gives you content for your website

- It gives you an opportunity to create additional products that come out of your book, such as courses, instructional materials, training and webinars

- It gives you content with which to create videos for YouTube and your website

- It gives you content with which to create a podcast

- It gives you content with which to create an audio book

- It gives you high value gifts that you can give to clients

- It gives you high value gifts that you can give to attendees at seminars, workshops and client events

- It brings in a new income stream

There are some other 'side benefits' to writing a book that should not be sniffed at:

- It makes you more organised

- Once your writing muscle starts to develop, it is hugely enjoyable as a process

- Your command of the English language expands

- Getting the idea of writing a book into your head, instinctively makes you think like a marketer

- You become better at research and more open to ideas

- People want to talk to you from a variety of walks of life

- You become in demand as a podcast guest and for other interviews

To my way of thinking, there are very few, if any downsides that could outweigh the benefits of writing a book. But in the interest of balance we should address common concerns that people have when it comes to putting pen to paper, such as:

- The time needed for the project
- What to write about
- Getting organised and actually getting started
- How to get published
- Is there a cost to this?
- Do I have sufficient expertise to write a book?

These are all valid points so let's take a look at some of them.

Firstly, there are a million and one people selling courses on how to write a book, so there is no shortage of advice out there. Just search for *How to Write a Book* on YouTube and you will find everything you need. There is no one right way to get started as an author.

The purpose of this book is to highlight why and how writing a book can support your marketing as a financial adviser, so I don't propose to go into the nuts and bolts of the actual writing. If you would like help with that, please drop me a line to philip@financialadvice.marketing and I can point you in the right direction, or indeed help you directly.

As to what you are going to write about, if you are still reading up to this point, there's a fair chance you might already even have an inkling of an idea at the back of your mind.

What is important is to clarify what we mean by a book.

When I suggest writing a book, most people instinctively think of something over an inch thick with three hundred or so pages. Actually, once you have got your head around the idea, a book of any size is very doable, but for most financial advisers something between eighty and two hundred pages will be perfect – particularly if it's your first book.

That's perfect too if you want to focus your book on either a niche or particular area of expertise. So for example a book called *The Complete Guide to Financial*

Planning is clearly going to be a lot more work than a book called (say) *Ten Easy Ways to Have More Money in Retirement*. In theory, a book with that title could be just ten pages in length. You get the idea.

But to produce something that you will be proud of and tick all of the benefit boxes above, you need to be looking at something around one hundred and eighty pages in length.

How long will that take?

Anything between a week and a year. But why rush it – take your time.

Do you have the expertise to write a book?

Yes, you're a financial adviser, and regardless of where you are in your career, you *can* do it. If you really do feel that you are not yet ready, or "not passed enough exams" as one adviser said to me, then another option is to work with another more experienced adviser. Make it a joint project.

A really important point to remember is not to make it hard for yourself. Unless you are highly experienced and have always fancied writing something substantial, then stick to what you know and try to make it niche. Another option is to write something for other advisers – perhaps telling something of your personal story.

Take a moment now to think about some very rough ideas of what, if push comes to shove, you could probably do something on. Try and come up with five rough ideas, topics or niches:

1.

2.

3.

4.

5.

And remember, most authors still do research before and during the writing process. Very few people 'know it all' and so still have to put some additional work in.

Getting organised

This is the hardest part; forcing yourself to stop procrastinating and actually start typing your first few words.

As I said, I don't propose to go into organising chapter headings etc. and putting it all in a logical order – there is plenty of information on that elsewhere. But at some point, you are going to be staring at a blank Word document (or whatever word processing package you use) and a blinking cursor.

It's also very likely that you will write a couple of paragraphs and then delete them in horror - and that will be accompanied by feelings of hopelessness and a desire to stop before it gets any harder. At this point, the thought of writing the best part of two hundred pages will seem impossible.

But this is a moment that everyone writing a book goes through, and a little faith and perseverance will keep you going. Once you get started and can keep going for about five minutes, your brain's desire to finish will start to kick in. Humans are hardwired to finish things we start – even if they do take a long time, so the act of starting and working for a few minutes will be enough to trigger that mechanism.

Aim to write for just fifteen minutes – set a timer on your phone. Then, stop and take a break for some fresh air. You will find that fifteen minutes will fly by.

Then go for another fifteen minutes, followed by another short break. Rinse and repeat but extend the writing period to twenty-five minutes.

Before you know it, you will have two or three pages written. It won't be perfect, but you will have started, and you will feel motivated to keep going.

For the first couple of days, stick to about ninety minutes maximum, but after that take as long as you wish, but stop when you feel tired or if the words just aren't coming out right.

My advice from there on is to write something every day. At the end of each chapter or however you are dividing up the content, read through it and make changes where it doesn't sound or feel quite right. A common issue you will find is that newer writers tend to be quite repetitive. At the time of writing have seventeen books to my name and I still find that I repeat myself – very often several times in the same paragraph! So this is an opportunity to go through and make changes. The synonym tool in your word processing package is your friend here.

In an ideal world, at the very end of the writing process you should have your text professionally proofread, and even then, if you are going down the traditional publisher route, it will go to an editor and at least two further proof-readers.

OK, that's enough on the process for now. My job is to convince you that writing a book is a good idea for a financial adviser and to get you started. The next question we need to answer is how we get your masterpiece out to the world.

To publish or not to publish…

At the end of the day, your book is a tool to enhance the perception of your expertise and to market yourself. However, your book needs to be marketed in its own right. There's little point in writing one if it is invisible to the world.

Or is there?

However, it may be that you don't want to have your book on the shelves of Waterstones, and that your goal was only to have something of value that you give to clients, or that you give away at your seminars and events. And that is perfectly fine as a strategy, because it is not compulsory to shout from the rooftops that you have a book (though I definitely would highlight it on your website as a key differentiator).

The cost of self-publishing and print-on-demand is peanuts today, so any expense in creating a book as a client gift is negligible in the scheme of things.

You generally have eight options to get your book out there:

- PDF eBook that you give away or sell to people (the simplest and easiest option)
- The above but printed out
- The above but printed using a professional printing service – either locally or online
- Printed through a traditional publisher
- Printed through Amazon KDP (Kindle Direct Publishing)
- Kindle eBook (and other eReaders)
- Printed through other print-on-demand services such as Lulu, IngramSpark etc.
- Audio version

The traditional publisher has typically been the default route for many years, but things are changing – or to be precise, there are now more options available.

I have two books through a traditional publisher, with the remainder all being self-published through Amazon. The latter are all available as real paperback books and as Kindle eBooks. The longest has 358 pages, with the shortest at 45, so you can see that within reason, anything goes – and that is the joy of self-publishing.

As to whether you go for a traditional publisher or self-publish, is entirely up to you. Each has its pros and cons, but from a business perspective as it relates to financial advisers, the easiest route is self-publishing through Amazon.

If you go through a traditional publisher, there is a critical extra step you almost always have to take – and that is before you write your book, you should write a *book proposal* which you use to pitch to publishers.

You can either send your proposal direct to publishers or you can go through a literary agent.

We've all heard about how authors have sent their book manuscript to multiple publishers only to have them rejected – the book proposal is designed to help improve your chances of acceptance. Only long-established authors and high-profile personalities can get away without writing a proposal, and even then, publishers need to be able to see why it will sell if they take it on.

I am certain that my first book was only accepted by the first publisher that I sent it to, because I wrote a detailed proposal pitching it to them.

Your proposal is your sales presentation to the publisher and covers:

- Why the book is needed
- How it is unique
- How it differs from others covering the same topic
- How you plan to promote it
- Why it will sell
- Etc.

Very often, even if a publisher rejects your proposal, they will give you reasons why, and this is invariably very useful information. Equally, even when they do accept your proposal, they will suggest ways and ideas to make the book even better.

What's more, there is a right way to put your proposal together. Again, precisely how you do that is outside the scope of this book, but I explain it in detail in my book *56 New Income Streams for Financial Advisers* at https://amzn.to/2CHyuRR

So a much simpler way to get your book out there is to self-publish. There are multiple videos on YouTube that can help you but is incredibly easy. Start by creating your account at Amazon KDP at https://kdp.amazon.com and follow the instructions.

They give you instructions on formatting your text, how to include images and then you decide whether you want a Kindle eBook or a paperback (or both).

You then upload your manuscript and cover art if you have it, or you can use a built-in tool to create your cover there and then within Amazon's system. Amazon will automatically assign an ISBN number for your paperback version.

Then you add some promotional text, some keywords and book categories and then the price you want to sell it at.

Amazon then takes up to seventy-two hours to approve it and advises you of any formatting errors etc.

From the moment of adding a new book within the Amazon system and uploading my manuscript, all of the above usually takes me about an hour. And of course, you can always hire someone to do *everything* for you through sites like Upwork, PeoplePerHour and Fiverr.

And yes, you can even hire people to ghost write the book for you for up to and around $300. But I would only recommend that if you are planning to create multiple (dozens) of books within a short period as a special project.

Having pressed the submit button, sit back and relax – you are nearly a published author.

And what does Amazon charge you for the privilege of hosting and printing your book?

Nothing – at least nothing up front. For every sale you make, Amazon will deduct a small cut from your royalties, and of course the cost of printing each book. Clearly the royalties you make on Kindle eBooks will be greater because there are no printing costs. You can also order author copies of your paperback books at cost price.

If you want to take things a stage further, Amazon offers a range of advertising and promotional packages to give your book greater visibility. However if your book starts selling and getting some good reviews, Amazon's algorithm will give your book greater visibility automatically.

In the meantime, there is something else you can do which will help to promote your book and add more credibility to your financial adviser brand, and that is to create an Amazon Author Page.

This is a page that anyone who has a book on Amazon can create. Again it is quick and simple to do, and once live, something you can point to from a variety of places:

- Your business cards
- Your email signature
- Your LinkedIn profile
- Twitter
- Facebook
- Your website
- Your blog, YouTube channel etc.

Here's what an Amazon Author Page looks like – and as you can see, it is a fantastic marketing platform: http://bit.ly/PhilipCalvertAmazon

If you have a particularly high number of followers on social media, Amazon can also give you your own 'shop front' such as this https://www.amazon.co.uk/shop/philipcalvert

In summary…

Clearly, I have made this all sound ridiculously easy, but here's the thing – it is! Truth be told, I procrastinated for ages about self-publishing, believing the whole process from thinking of an idea to unboxing your first books to be difficult, longwinded and technically tricky. It was only when I finally pulled my finger out and watched a few YouTube videos that I started to kick myself at how easy this is.

The point?

As we said at the beginning of this chapter, writing a book is an incredibly powerful way for financial advisers to market themselves and their expertise. The hardest part will be believing that you can actually do it and putting pen to paper - but just making a start will get you there, and the moment when you give your first copy away to a client or when you start seeing sales coming in through the Amazon dashboard, is one of those great life moments.

Grab the opportunity to enjoy one of those moments – *and* enhance the perception of your financial advice business's expertise, credibility and professionalism at the same time.

The Power and the Story

Tell Stories in your Marketing

The acclaimed author Philip Pullman once said, *"After nourishment, shelter and companionship, stories are the thing we need most in the world."*

I've heard others also saying that humans are hardwired to listen to stories. When we lived in caves, at the end of the day we didn't sit round watching Netflix; we did the next best thing – tell stories. Stories handed down through generations, that captivated our attention and put our imaginations to work.

Stories are incredibly powerful at helping humans to connect with one another, and they are a proven technique to engage your audience when presenting at your seminars and client events. That's one of the main reasons why seminars are so effective as a marketing strategy.

Note also that Facebook uses 'Stories' as a key product on its main platform and on Instagram – opportunities to share quick snippets of your day to day life. Love or hate Facebook, the Stories product has very quickly become central to the world of social media.

Two things come out of this which are important for financial advisers.

Firstly, we live in a world where attention spans are getting shorter and shorter. Watch as people flit rapidly from one status update to another, and then another – and then another. Before you know if you have been scrolling endlessly on your mobile device for hours and achieved nothing. We are all guilty of it to a greater or lesser degree.

Again, our clients and prospects do it too – and not just youngsters. On trains and planes and in restaurants and bars I have witnessed baby boomers and much older, scrolling endlessly on tablets and iPhones.

According to an article in the Observer Technology section, Simon Parkin recounted the following:

In an unprecedented attack of candour, Sean Parker, the 38-year-old founding president of Facebook, recently admitted that the social network was founded not to unite us, but to distract us. "The thought process was: 'How do we consume as much of your time and conscious attention as possible?'"

He continued:

To achieve this goal, Facebook's architects exploited a "vulnerability in human psychology", explained Parker, who resigned from the company in 2005. Whenever someone likes or comments on a post or photograph, he said, "we... give you a little dopamine hit".

I'm no neuroscientist, but I've read similar posts from 'real' brain experts who broadly agree. So broadly speaking, much of social media can be addictive, particularly if you have an addictive personality.

But the point for us as marketers is that our prospects are glued to their devices. True, they are not all on social media, but one way or another all roads lead to Facebook, Twitter, YouTube et al.

So how do we interrupt them? How do we get their attention when they are online? And how do we get them to click on our post or link ahead of everyone else's?

One way is as we have described earlier – to create our own 'addictive' content through our own social networking groups – online communities etc., so that it becomes habit forming for them to engage with us and other members just like themselves. Remember, people are naturally drawn to others who are like us and who share common interests and stories.

Or, we design our marketing content in such a way that it rapidly grabs people's attention. It HAS to stand out from the crowd – just as we do as businesses.

Ask yourself, in your Facebook ads or titles for your blogs, are you making your key point CLEAR to your target market very quickly? Because if you're not, that short attention span just isn't going to linger on your online content. And before you know it, it's gone.

If they like what they see and it grabs their attention, then they may well go on to do something else that is very common today – binge on your content.

Time and time again I'm asked at workshops how to get attention on LinkedIn, and apart from a few tricks which play to the LinkedIn algorithm, more often than not attention comes from GREAT copywriting. And specifically the headline you use for your article, blog or status update.

Who remembers this?

WORLD WAR TWO BOMBER FOUND ON THE MOON

Ah, the heady days of the Sunday Sport from April 24th 1988; that never to be forgotten headline that got the nation talking.

And that's the point – the headline grabbed our attention and up went sales. Newspaper editors have been doing it for years and there is direct correlation between the quality and creativity of the headline and the sales on a given day.

Now, clearly there is a difference between marketing a financial planning business and marketing a cheap Sunday newspaper, but you get my drift. Your headlines are everything, and in this strange social media world, we need to get attention – and fast.

Even for our high quality content such as articles that are written for a local newspaper or our website, people's attention spans are shorter than ever, and if the title doesn't get their attention quickly, they will miss out on a potentially valuable and important piece of personal finance information.

Once you do have their attention, you need to keep it, and the best way to do that is to write stories. So yes, put effort and professionalism into your articles, blogs and videos, but get professional with your headlines too.

An excellent book I can recommend on this is *Copywriting Secrets* by Jim Edwards – one of the world's

leading exponents of the art. Get yours at
https://amzn.to/36DQGcs

The second point that is important for financial advisers is how when a story is associated with a product or service, the perceived value of that product or service can be increased and made even more appealing. Again, another reason why it is important to tell stories when presenting at seminars.

Significant Objects was a literary and anthropological experiment devised by New York Times freelance journalist Rob Walker and author Joshua Glenn, which demonstrated that the effect of narrative on any given object's subjective value can be measured objectively.

The project was to auction off cheap, random, often tacky thrift-store objects via eBay. Walker and Glenn commissioned over a hundred creative writers to create short stories as the item descriptions accompanying the objects being sold.

Before being advertised for sale on eBay, the objects were purchased for $1.25 each on average, and went on to be sold for significantly more when accompanied by a short fictional story.

For example:

- A choirboy figurine was purchased for $1.99 and sold on eBay for $21.50

- A white mug with a marines logo on it (printed upside down) was purchased for 75 cents and sold on eBay for $37

- An Indian Squaw figurine was purchased for 99 cents and sold for $157.50

- A bubble bath teapot was purchased for $1 and sold for $59

- A globe paperweight was purchased for $1.49 and sold on eBay later for $197.50

In each case, the object was presented for sale along with a fictional story that related to the object, and the experiment proves that humans are drawn to, connect with and resonate with stories.

The book of the Significant Objects experiment is well worth a read: https://amzn.to/2QzJloE. One of the five-star reviews sums it up nicely:

"An experiment that provides real, specific examples on how the power of storytelling increases an object's value. Substitute the word "object" with "brand" and you've got yourself a book on content marketing. Recommended for anyone in the applied storytelling/content marketing fields."

The lessons for financial advisers in their marketing?

- Avoid stats, numbers and data

- People buy people – and their stories

- Avoid industry jargon

- Use case studies that feature real people and clients

- Create marketing content that informs and entertains

- Avoid talking about yourself – talk about how real people with real problems and issues have been helped by you

- When you do talk about yourself – tell it as a story; how you came to be who you are, what shaped you and your values, struggles you overcame etc.

- Be much more creative in your 'About us' text on your website. Tell a story – even better have a short film made. There's more on this in a later chapter

Summary

- People have short attention spans online – including our prospects

- Get their attention with great headlines, titles and copywriting

- Tell stories in your communications – whether live in person or in your online content

- Stories don't have to be five pages long. They can be just as equally be two sentences which are the launchpad into describing who you are, what you believe or the way you help people. They can be a moment in time that changed everything for you

Working the Room

Networking

We have mentioned networking a couple of times in this book, but mostly *online* networking. There are still multiple benefits to face-to-face networking but my research amongst thousands of financial advisers suggests that only around 10% make time to regularly attend networking events, with much of their networking done 'accidentally'.

Yes, there is a lot of networking done within the financial advice profession at industry events, but what I'm talking about is within your local community where you meet people who are not advisers, paraplanners or suppliers.

The benefits are:

- Social media is fine up to a point, but people like to see the whites of your eyes

- Closer relationships build more quickly around common interests when face-to-face than when meeting online

- Trust builds faster when meeting face-to-face, making it more likely that the relationship will build quicker

- You become referable sooner in the relationship than when online

- It is an opportunity to showcase your personality

- Body language comes into play and speaks much louder than words on a screen

- Tone of voice adds to the communication mix and influences how you are perceived

- Chemistry can be built upon when face-to-face

- There is less room for overreaction and misinterpretation of messages when face-to-face

- Magic, luck, serendipity (whatever you want to call it) happens when you get out there

And if you target businesspeople as a financial adviser, it seems that face-to-face communication is preferred much more than online. A survey by Forbes that asked 760 business executives revealed that 84% preferred face-to-face communication. Of those, 85% cited that it builds stronger, more meaningful business relationships.

Respondents also said that face-to-face meetings are best for persuasion (91%), leadership (87%), and engagement (86%).

I'm the first to say that financial advisers should be making far better use of technology for communications but being seen live and in person is unbeatable.

The problem is most of us have never been taught how to network. When in the corporate world I attended training courses on presentation skills, dealing with the media, customer services, face to face sales, key account management and customer service – but never networking and how to network.

We've all seen the worst type of networkers, haven't we...

They're usually to be found at larger networking events, where they sneak into the room before everyone else and leave their business card on every chair they can find. They are the equivalent of many businesspeople on social media – they are only interested in themselves, their voice and their wallet.

True, when any of us takes time out to attend a networking event, we are giving up valuable time in the hope that something positive might come out of it. And unfortunately that is why networking doesn't really work for most people, because we are thinking only of ourselves.

The best networkers look at it the other way round and go to networking events with the sole intention of trying to help other people, and with the expectation of receiving absolutely nothing in return.

Ultimately networking is about connecting, introducing and referring people, so here are three questions that you can use that will put you in the big league of networkers. You will also see a remarkable turnaround in the value you get from attending networking events.

Firstly, instead of asking that same old, same old question *"What do you do?"*, ask,

"What is your area of expertise?"

It's a great question to be asked because it makes you believe that the person asking already thinks you are an expert on something.

When you have asked the question, look at the other person in the eye and just listen. Don't try to feel the need to interrupt. Let them talk.

Next question to ask is,

"What are you working on in your business right now that's a key project?"

Or,

"What's happening in your business right now that's really important to you?"

Or,

"What's the big issue that you are working on in your business right now?"

Again, let them answer in as much detail as they will let you have.

The final question is,

"Who could I connect you to who could be useful to you in your work?"

Or, ask it in another way depending on how they answered your second question.

"If I could introduce you to anyone who could help bring the project in faster, cheaper etc, what sort of connection would be useful to you?"

You can create your own versions of the questions, but essentially you are asking *"What sort of help would be useful to you if I could find it for you?"*

These questions are clearly not about you – they are about the other person. They are also about connecting people to the help they need, and with the expectation of receiving nothing in return.

As a financial adviser, there is a fair chance that when you ask the second question of *"What's the big issue that you are working on in your business right now?"*, at the back of your mind you'll be hoping that they will say,

"That's easy – we're trying to find someone who could set up a new pension and employee benefits package for our staff"

That's not going to happen!

The chances are that their answer will be something fairly banal or ordinary such as,

"We're trying to find a reliable photocopier supplier", or

"We really could do with a specialist accountant who can help us with our new international work."

You know the sort of thing. But now it's over to you, and unless you can think of a contact there and then, you should aim to get back to them the following day having had time to think about it, ask around or look through your LinkedIn connections.

Even if you can't find what they are looking for, you should still get back to them, saying that it was great to meet them, but that on this occasion you can't help. If anything does come up, you'll be sure to get in touch.

Regardless of whether you can or can't help them, they will still be grateful for your efforts and you will have made a new contact whom you tried to help – and they won't forget it.

Introducing people to others is at the heart of great networking. Just as you often rely on people referring contacts to your financial advice services (and are presumably extremely grateful), you too should always be looking for ways to help other people in this way. And when you do, they will never forget you.

In short, networking is about connecting and making connections and introductions. Whenever you go to an event (industry or otherwise), look for opportunities to connect people to the help they need – and do it with the expectation of nothing in return.

But before long, you will be referred to as 'a great networker', and with that comes many rewards, with people instinctively wanting to refer contacts to you.

The more you give – the more you will get.

See you in the Pub

Start your own Networking group

In addition to informal networking at events, you can also join more formal networking groups – for example BNI (Business Network International).

There are multiple benefits of joining your local BNI, which they summarise as follows:

- Increase Business Prospects: You'll substantially increase your business through referrals

- Professional Development: You'll have access to our exclusive training programs and opportunities to sharpen your presentation and business skills

- Great Networking Opportunities: Your participation in up to 50 networking meetings per year will increase your exposure to many other business professionals in your community

- Exclusive Member Resources: You'll have access to a range of tools and educational materials on networking, public speaking and business best-practices

So it's clear that organisations like BNI have much to offer a local financial adviser, but whilst many find membership to be hugely beneficial, it is not for everyone.

There are of course other networking organisations (such as NRG Networks) that you could join – in fact any type of networking will have its benefits if you commit to it.

But an alternative being explored by a number of financial advisers around the UK and wider world, is to set up their own local networking group.

This is easier than it sounds and has three core benefits:

1. Your group can be targeted at potentially any type of audience, but is particularly valuable when the financial adviser has a target market of small businesses, entrepreneurs, business owners and executives in local companies

2. Your group positions you as a key business resource

3. You build community around your brand

In turn, these result in you,

- Getting more referrals
- Enlarging your circle of connections
- Becoming seen as the local connector – a 'go to' person
- Getting names for your newsletter
- Benefiting from on demand help and advice
- Having a positive influence on others
- Building new friendships
- Making money (depending on the model you adopt)

You can make your networking events as simple or as complicated as you wish. At its most basic, all you need to do is to tell a few local business connections that from next month, and thereafter the first Thursday of every month, you will be in the back room of the local pub or hotel where there will be drinks, nibbles and networking from 5.30pm.

The emphasis will be on networking and meeting others. You could give a short presentation or speech or invite a local businessperson to say a few words. Then it's back to the drinks and nibbles.

That's it. And as part of your welcome presentation, you point out that it is going to be same time and place next month.

Aim small to start with – if you can get just five people to attend your first event, you have done well. And start with people you already know so that conversation flows easily.

Play around with the format to suit you, but something along these lines works well:

- Start at 5.30pm with drinks and nibbles

- Have a team member give out badges to attendees with your logo. Maybe even brand the event – it's up to you

- Formally welcome people at (say) 6.15pm – talk for ten minutes to say what the objectives are

- If it's a small group, ask people to introduce themselves – maybe highlight an opportunity or challenge they have, or even to say what help or connections they are looking for at the moment

- Guest speaker or presenter for twenty to thirty minutes – this could be you, one of the attendees or someone else

- Thank everyone for attending and explain that you will be doing it again next month

- Back to the bar.

Bear in mind that you can play around with the format – for example hold it outside during the summer months.

Whatever you do, keep it simple – there is no need to over complicate things. In due course you can set up a simple website or even a section on your own site to promote the event. This is recommended because over time Google will index your pages so that it becomes visible to local people and businesses.

You can also promote it on Facebook through a special Page, and you can use LinkedIn's events tool too. Twitter and Instagram will also be useful for promotions. Create and use your own dedicated hashtag in all your social media promotions and encourage attendees to use it when they are at the event.

If you want to get fancy, use a booking tool like Eventbrite. Naturally, this all comes at a cost – not least of which is your time – but it will be time very well spent, and you are all but guaranteed that you will have conversations that lead somewhere, not just for you but everyone who attends.

In terms of tangible costs, you will need to fund the first event, possibly even the first two or three. But essentially you will just be paying for a few drinks and nibbles and some promotion – but even then, it won't take much to get half a dozen attendees. Fund it while it is still small!

So during your welcome remarks, you could say that this first group will be considered as founder members who can attend for free for the first six months, as long as they can invite or encourage their contacts to attend in future. Ideally you need to be charging for attendance but find a way to incentivise these early adopters to help you with the promotions.

Make sure that you take photos and send a Press Release to your local papers. Maybe even invite a local journalist to come along to the next one – this is potentially GREAT PR for you. Take some video too, featuring thirty to sixty second clips for your website and promotional activities. In particular, try to get testimonials for the event on video.

Get a couple of pull-up banners made which are in the meeting room, and which will be seen in photos and video of the event.

Send out a follow up email, which in time can become a regular newsletter – again all branded with your business.

Clearly this all takes a little planning, but hopefully you can see that the underlying idea and concept is very simple, but which has big benefits for you and your business.

Ultimately, this is a giving activity. You are creating a friendly environment for local people to come together, to network and help each other out – with you and your business positioned at the centre. Over time, it will grow and become a valuable networking hub in your community. Yes, you may well outgrow your venue, but that's not a problem to concern yourself at the outset.

When you do start selling out each event, then you can start thinking about either capping membership making it even more appealing) or moving elsewhere. That will be a nice problem to have…

Remember, this is all about creating community and value around you. You are providing something of potentially very high value to your target audience, and so will reflect very positively on you and your brand.

New Kid on the Blog

Blogging

W e have mentioned blogs a few times in this book, so it's time to highlight blogging in its own right.

In an interview for Inc.com, international marketing authority and author of the acclaimed personal branding book *"KNOWN: The Handbook for Building and Unleashing your Personal Brand in the Digital Age"* Mark Schaefer said,

"Determining influence is so critical to brands because this is what drives word of mouth validation – typically the most powerful and cost-effective marketing method available."

Again, we come back to word of mouth and referrals, and yet it still amazes me how few financial advisers write a regular blog, particularly in the UK. Most have considered it or even written a few posts but left it there.

Blogging is something you need to commit to, and whilst this can be time consuming, the benefits are phenomenal. Here are a few:

- Positions you as an expert in your field or on a particular topic

- Google scrapes up your content and shows it in search results

- Blogging can be done on multiple platforms – including everything from your website to LinkedIn

- Blogs can be repurposed into other types of content – podcasts, videos, eGuides and even books that can be sold

- Blogging differentiates you from other advisers – particularly locally

- Blogging can attract speaking bookings – both paid and free, but which showcase your expertise

- Writing a blog will attract podcast hosts and radio stations who want to interview you

- A blog can get you on television interviews

- A blog is a great way to add value to existing clients

- You often get immediate feedback from your readers, which can lead to valuable conversations

- A blog keeps you front of mind with your professional introducers

- Blogging dramatically improves your writing skills

- Blogging helps people to get to know you as a person

- Blogging grows your professional network, builds your online identity and trust

- Blogging can dramatically increase your email list for newsletters etc.

- Your blog can often become the foundation for a business in its own right

As blogging expert Nick Scheidies says,

"A blog can be more than just a way of advancing your online presence; it can be a way of advancing your life... a platform you create that can propel you forward in the direction of your choice."

Here a few ideas to make sure your blog captures hearts and minds:

- Be consistent. Commit and post at the same time every day, week or month. But don't post at the expense of quality. Make sure it is something you are proud to share

- Be guided by your audience – answer their questions in your blog and write about what they want to read. Yes, do some research

- Use highly compelling titles to catch attention

- Remember – your blog is not a sales letter. It is there to add value, inform and occasionally entertain. But do remember to include keywords that you want to get found for on Google

- Capture the email addresses of readers so that you can communicate with them outside your blog – ask for feedback, opinions and ideas. Give them bonuses and freebies to keep them engaged

- As a postscript at the end of each blog, give a brief 'trailer' or insight into what will be in the next post. Make them curious about what is coming next

- Always include a call to action such as signing up for your newsletter or to follow you on Twitter, or even to connect on LinkedIn

- Include social sharing tools, so that readers can quickly and easily post snippets or links to their own followers. Most commercial blogging platforms include these tools

- Show people behind the scenes of your life and business. People usually find that hugely compelling

- Mention other experts and high-profile bloggers in your blog – and later reach out to them and point them to where you have mentioned them. Often they will then highlight your blog in their own content, which inevitably gets you more readers. (Search "Influencer marketing" on Google for information on how best to do this and be sure to read the later chapter 'The Dream 100')

- Be yourself – don't feel that you have to write in a certain way. Just because you are a financial adviser doesn't mean that you have to be technical or overtly 'professional'. Show something of you in your writing

- Make a note of the blogs which get the most likes, shares, conversations or interaction. These are clues as to what your audience wants to see more of

- Be patient – blogging is not an overnight thing

So, it is clear that blogging has much going for it. When will you start yours?

For many people who are thinking about writing a blog, their thoughts inevitably swirl around *"What will I write about?"* or *"How will I find the time?"* or *"Won't I run out of ideas to write about?"* And imposter syndrome is likely to creep in too.

Like any new activity, it takes time to get into the swing of it and to make it a habit. You may well write three paragraphs and then give up, but stick with it.

It doesn't take long to find your groove – particularly when you focus on what you know, like and understand.

Always carry a notebook with you so that when ideas pop into your head you can jot them down. After a while a radar switches on in your head which constantly scans your world for ideas, and before you know it you have enough bullet points for several weeks or months' worth of content.

Your clients are also a great source of content for blogs. Case studies are essentially stories, and stories make compelling reading – particularly if they have relevance to individual readers.

Remember, all of the top bloggers started with a blank page and no readers.

A final point about consistency; once you start blogging it is very important that you keep going – particularly if you host your blog on your website. There is nothing worse for a website visitor than visiting your blog page to find just three posts, or to see that the last one was written two years ago.

So, yes blogging is a commitment, but hopefully you can see that it is very much worth it.

~

If you have not read Mark Schaefer's book *"Known"* mentioned above, I highly recommend it – not least because it features a case study on Pete Matthew – financial planner at Jacksons Wealth Management in Cornwall.

Vlog 'til you Drop

Vlogging

Video Blogging is the next logical step on from Blogging – instead of writing your content, you film it and post regularly on a video hosting/sharing platform such as YouTube or Vimeo.

Why blog on video? The figures speak for themselves. According to tubularinsights, marketers who use video grow revenue 49% faster than non-video users. Sixty-four percent of consumers make a purchase after watching branded social videos.

And the video making platform Biteable shares statistics from major internet platforms:

- 81% of businesses use video as a marketing tool — up from 63% over the last year. (Hubspot)

- 6 out of 10 people would rather watch online videos than television. (Google)

- Mobile video consumption rises by 100% every year. (Insivia)

- By 2022, online videos will make up more than 82% of all consumer internet traffic - 15 times higher than it was in 2017. (Cisco)

- 78% of people watch online videos every week, and 55% view online videos every day. (HubSpot)

- YouTube is the second most popular website after Google. (Alexa)

- Users view more than 1 billion hours of video each day on YouTube. (YouTube)

- 59% of executives say they would rather watch a video than read text. (Wordstream)

- 75% of all video plays are on mobile devices. (eMarketer)

- Viewers retain 95% of a message when they watch it in a video, compared to 10% when reading it in text. (Insivia)

- 72% of customers would rather learn about a product or service by way of video. (HubSpot)

- 92% of users watching video on mobile will share it with others. (Wordstream)

- By 2020 there will be close to 1 million minutes of video crossing the internet per second. (Cisco)

So the video usage statistics are compelling, but does it work from a marketing perspective? Biteable continues:

- Videos attract 300% more traffic and help to nurture leads. (MarketingSherpa)

- A website is 53 times more likely to reach the front page of Google if it includes video. (Insivia)

- Including a video on your landing page can boost your conversion rate by up to 80%. (Unbounce)

- Nearly 50% of internet users look for videos related to a product or service before visiting a store. (Hubspot)

- Video increases organic search traffic on a website by 157%. (Conversion XL)

- 85% of consumers want to see more video content from brands. (HubSpot)

- 65% of executives have gone to the marketer's site and 39% have called them on the phone after watching a marketing video. (Forbes)

- 97% of marketers say video has helped users gain a better understanding of their products and services. (Hubspot)

- 52% of marketers say video is the type of content with the best ROI. (HubSpot)

- Adding video to your emails can increase click rates by 300%. (HubSpot)

- On average, people spend 2.6x more time on pages with video than without. (Wistia)

Yet...

Whenever I mention using video to financial advisers at workshops, I often see arms being crossed and an inevitable hand goes up accompanied by the question, *"What about compliance? They won't allow video."*

I normally reply by saying,

"Have you ever asked them?"

The answer is usually *"No, I haven't."*

It is true to say that different compliance teams have different attitudes to social media and the sharing of content. At one end of the scale, compliance teams simply give the following guidance:

Do what you like on social media, but

- **Don't do financial promotions**
- **Don't give financial advice, and**
- **Don't bring the company into disrepute**

To my way of thinking, this is a perfectly sensible approach, particularly when accompanied by random sampling of an adviser's social media posts each quarter.

At the other end of the scale, some compliance teams take the approach of saying that every single post –

even if it is a tweet about the latest football results – has to be pre-approved.

Others take a halfway house approach of saying that advisers can post anything from a set of pre-approved financial services related content, through to anything personal or 'non-FS' content that they wish.

In my view, it is only a matter of time until financial advice firms, large and small will have little choice in using video to educate, inspire and inform consumers if for no other reason than the competition will be using it as a standard part of their communications.

In short, we, as a profession will miss out massively if we don't embrace video.

From talking to advisers who do successfully use video with little, if any input or 'interference' from their compliance teams, I have noted the following best practice.

Financial education videos – two to four minutes maximum explaining what a product or concept is. For example, a simple guide to Income Replacement Insurance. What it is, how it works, who should consider taking it out etc.

Newspaper reviews – a weekly video on a Monday morning where an adviser talks through or reviews three articles that they saw in the personal finance pages of the weekend press. The adviser chooses articles that are relevant to their target audience, and simply highlights what was included, what they agreed with, maybe what they didn't agree with and then adds any thoughts of his or her own that may have been missed.

The video can then be hosted on the adviser's YouTube or Vimeo channel and an email sent to their newsletter list. This way you get to post regular content which is valuable, but which highlights the adviser as the expert (not the journalist who wrote it).

Sections from your seminars – this is an easy one. When you run or host a seminar or event, show short sections of the content that you presented. This highlights your expertise and reminds people that you also run seminars.

Sections from your client events – more and more advisers are hosting client appreciation events these days, so these are great opportunities to get video snippets for posting online.

Sections from your networking events – see the previous sections on networking.

Case studies – simply talk about a real or fictitious client case study. Highlight the key issues and how you approached it.

Client testimonials – as mentioned previously, client testimonials on video are some of the most powerful and impactful marketing a financial adviser can do.

Meet the team – another really simple way to produce a video; simply chat with people in your office. Keep it friendly and relaxed and give your prospects the opportunity to get to know people who work with you.

Behind the Scenes – again a really simple one where you follow the process of what happens during the financial planning process. This one often proves to be extremely valuable, because many people don't really know what a financial planner does, so this behind the scenes insight will be useful to them when deciding which adviser firm to work with.

Client Q&A – a great source of content for your videos will be questions. In each episode, simply answer a question that has been asked by a client. It's a good idea to build up a bank of questions that are asked by clients and prospects and use these in your videos. If you can't already think about questions that you could use, have a brainstorming session with your team and come up with as many as you can. From today, commit to writing down every question that you are asked and use them in future videos.

Another good source of questions that people ask about personal finance is the Quora website. You can also look at a site called Answer the Public. Take a look at https://answerthepublic.com – type in a keyword like 'Pensions' and see all the questions that are being asked on search engines.

Expert interviews – just as you might do in a podcast, interview experts of interest for your YouTube channel. These experts could also be local businesspeople, and as well as adding value to your channel, you are also giving them publicity, to which they will doubtless want to reciprocate in due course through referrals.

Technical explanations – whilst this book goes to great pains to say that 'people buy people', many elements of financial advice and planning are highly technical. There will be some viewers of your video channel who will love to watch technical explanations – perhaps around tax etc. This gives them the opportunity to also get a sense of your expertise and it may even prompt questions and referrals.

Other ideas I've seen being used include:

- A day in the life of you or a client

- Before and after – a client's situation before and after they worked with you

- Friday shout out – every Friday you post a short video thanking someone who has helped you or your business over the last seven days

- Charity – post short videos updating people on a local charity or cause that you are supporting

- Time Lapse – if you have a building project taking place at your office, create a time lapse video

- Share client survey results

- Monthly client prize draw reveal

- Bloopers

In summary, there is much that goes on in the day to day life of a financial advice business. Think about how you could transfer some of what happens onto a video.

And finally a few points that are proven to make your videos more engaging:

Give your videos compelling titles that you might once have seen in the Classified Ads section of a newspaper or magazine – such as "How to…", "How I…", "Secrets of…", "5 Secrets of…", "Don't do this until you watch this" etc.

Add a 'trailer' on the home page of your YouTube channel which includes who you are, what you are about, how often you post, why they should subscribe, what they will get and exactly what you want them to do. You may even want to occasionally post a trailer for a series of videos that you are going to be running.

Always include a call to action in your videos – particularly to Like and Subscribe to your channel. This could also include inviting them to visit your website, call for information or sign up for your email newsletter. Never assume that your viewers will automatically Like, Share, Subscribe and Comment – you need to consciously tell them to do it.

Whilst you will have your own ideas for video content, your followers, fans and subscribers will also have their own ideas. Listen to what they have to say (often in the comments under a video) and also post what they want to see more of. This equally applies to your written blog, podcast and any other content that you put out.

Be consistent – if you have posted a dozen videos and you are getting very little traction, don't give up now! This is a long-haul activity, but one which you will not regret over time. Again, this also applies to blogging and podcasting.

What about the technical side of video?

All too often, it is not the compliance side of things that puts off financial advisers from using video – it is the technical aspects.

There tends to be a fear that this is going to require expensive cameras and specialist film making skills. In fact, quite the opposite is the case. Every financial adviser has all the technical equipment they need already in their pocket.

The key thing is to just get started.

I'll say it again...

Just get started.

Do something.

Get your phone out, prop it up in front of you or ask someone to point it at you and answer these three questions:

Who are you?

What do you do?

Who do you work with?

That's it.

It could take anything from thirty seconds to three minutes to do, but you will have done it.

Don't worry about the lighting or the sound or the editing; the whole point is to do something.

The more you do it, the better you will get and the more confident you will feel.

Pete Matthew and his YouTube channel Meaningful Money is a classic example of this. He posted his first videos almost ten years ago, and by his own admission the first ones were 'cheap and cheerful', but over time they have propelled him to be a leading exponent of sound and video amongst the financial advice profession.

Yes, today his level of technical proficiency is significantly different, but Pete will be the first to tell you that even when he was posting early more 'amateurish' videos, **each one had real value for his viewers** – and that's what really counts.

Take a look at his channel at https://www.youtube.com/user/MeaningfulMoney

One thing worth noting is that he has divided his videos into playlists, where he has categorised his content. These include:

- Millennial finance
- Equity release
- Advanced investing
- Life stages
- Long term care planning
- Working with a financial adviser
- UK taxes and tax planning
- Etc.

You could do the same or even use the ideas I've listed earlier.

Feeling nervous and self-conscious about recording your first video?

Guess what – so did everyone the first time they pressed the Record button. Like anything new it will feel a little uncomfortable at first, but you will soon get used to it – and as soon as you see your first few videos going live, you will wonder why you didn't do it ages ago.

But here are a few practical tips to help you get started.

- Jot down a few ideas for topics from the list we gave you earlier – go with the one you feel most comfortable with.

- Write down precisely who your video will be aimed at. This is important because it will give you far greater focus in your delivery.

- Write a script. Yes, for your first few videos, you will find it much easier if you know exactly what you are going to say in advance. In due course you will present your videos without a script, but to begin with let's make it easy for yourself.

- Keep the script short. Aim for three minutes maximum.

- Either print it out and read it, or use a teleprompter app. There are many to choose from in the various app stores – and most are free.

- If you feel uncomfortable reading a script, write out bullet points. Whether you use a script or bullet points, rehearse your delivery several times so that you become used to the material. The more you rehearse, the easier it will become, and you will probably end up not needing your prompts at all.

- Decide in advance to record your video several times. It's only going to be three minutes maximum, so it won't be very time consuming. Then, pick the one you are most happy with.

- Remember, it won't be perfect! Just get it done and put it live.

- Show the recordings to a friend or colleague to see what feedback they have – they might spot something you have forgotten or missed.

- Still too nervous to be on camera yourself? Turn your bullet points into a PowerPoint presentation and record yourself speaking over the slides. You can do that within PowerPoint itself, or use simple screen recording software such as Loom, Screencastify or Camtasia. You could even run it as a webinar on Zoom which you record.

- If you want to use something a little more fancy than PowerPoint, then consider using stock video footage that relates to the topic of your presentation.

- Finally, a great way to be on camera without having to 'present' on a topic, is to be interviewed by someone else who asks you pre-determined questions that relate to your bullet points.

So you can see that there are a variety of ways to get started with video content.

One of the best I have seen is Mike, an IFA in central London who was extremely nervous about using video. He wasn't comfortable putting himself in front of the camera, he wanted the production values to be high but didn't want to hire a videographer and he was really uncertain about the content he wanted to present. But like many advisers, he knew he needed to do something.

In the end, Mike just got up from his desk, walked into the corridor, switched on the camera on his phone and started talking.

And for the next five minutes he walked to the lifts, stepped in, walked outside the office and went down to a local coffee bar – all the while talking about something relating to personal finance that he had seen on the news that morning. It was a topic that had come up a number of times with his clients, so he knew they would find it interesting; what's more it was a topic he was passionate about and in which he had expertise.

Mike's video was completely unscripted and done in one take as he walked to get his morning coffee. Simple and effective, but most importantly got him started.

And for the avoidance of doubt, there was no financial advice being given and no financial promotion either – just his personal observations on something that he and his clients cared about.

He doesn't post every day, but about once a week as and when the mood takes him – but the format is always the same, with him walking out of his office and down to the coffee shop whilst talking to his phone.

I asked Mike if he felt self-conscious about walking around recording his video in the office and down the street. His answer was that he didn't, because he was talking about something he cared about – adding that when he reaches the street, everyone else seems to be doing the same thing!

The videos are far from 'perfect' technically, but that really doesn't matter. The idea is that you are not producing a BBC documentary – this is content that comes straight from the heart. The fact that Mike combines them with his morning walk to the coffee shop, gives the regular viewer a predictable and consistent framework to follow. They know how long the video is going to be and importantly they also get to feel that they 'know' Mike and something behind the scenes of his work.

Creating a framework or a theme for your videos is a great idea. You may remember from earlier that I mentioned Jim Edwards who is one of the world's leading marketing copywriters. He has a large property in Virginia and each day records a three to five-minute video about business and marketing as he walks from his house, down to feed and let out his chickens. He calls the video series "Letting the Chickens out with Jim".

Whatever the weather, Jim walks down his yard talking to camera. We then enter his chicken coup with him whilst he continues to share his thoughts and ideas for the day. The viewer always hears the chickens getting louder as Jim approaches and we also get glances of them scratching about. Simple, effective, intriguing and fun.

Our adviser friend Mike now also transcribes his videos and posts them as blogs. And yes, he is already mindful that after a few more videos and transcriptions, he will have sufficient material to create a book.

In short, try not to get put off by the perceived compliance, technical or presentational aspects of video. It always feels like it's a much bigger deal than it actually is, but if you were to talk to any independent marketing consultant about what is hot, works and gets traffic to your website, they will more than likely include video near the top of their list.

"A bio so good you could make it a movie"

Video Profiles

P lease bear with me while I stick with video for a little longer – but in a way that you might not have thought about.

A lot of people know that I do a party-piece at events where I can write the *About Us* page of their website for just about any financial adviser in the UK. And I can do it without having met them…

How?

Because the vast majority of advisers' *About Us* pages all say much the same thing.

This is a real example and is fairly typical [names have been changed]:

"James Miller joined County Wealth Management in June 2009. Prior to this, he gained valuable experience from an advisory firm in the City and one of the UK's most well-known private banks.

James has been awarded the CISI Level 4 Diploma in Investment Advice (Financial Planning & Advice) and will be focusing on business development and advising existing clients."

Then, thinking that it needs to have a more human touch, an adviser will often add something extra like this:

"Passionate about health and fitness, James enjoys being a member at CrossFit Academy because of its buzzing atmosphere and variety of high intensity workouts.

At weekends, James likes walking in the countryside with his wife (weather permitting!) and tasting different gins!"

I have shown this example at over twenty different presentations around the UK, and at every one of them, there was usually one financial adviser in the audience who laughed out loud saying something like *"That's my actual profile!"*

Much the same thing happens on LinkedIn. Every year LinkedIn releases a list of the most over-used buzzwords on members' profiles. Here is the latest:

Creative

Organisational

Effective

Extensive experience

Track record

Strategic

Proven sales professional

Leadership

Dynamic

Motivated

Innovative

Passionate

Problem solving

Expert

Exceptional communication skills

At marketing workshops, I ask advisers to cross check the list against their own LinkedIn profile, and time and time again they find that many are using the exact same words.

Look at that list again and ask yourself where those words are usually to be found?

Yes, a CV.

We mentioned earlier how Michael Kitces describes the financial advice community as having a crisis of differentiation, and in my view the examples of website *About Us* pages and the words we use to highlight our expertise and value on LinkedIn tend to go towards proving the point.

A few years ago, my eighty-something mother-in-law Beryl moved near to us and needed a financial adviser. Her actual words to me were:

"Can we go on your internet thingy and find someone who can help me?"

I already knew several top-quality IFA firms in our village but thought it better that we did the search together whilst also spreading the net a little wider than the immediate five square miles.

So we did, and searched "Financial Adviser in Guildford"

Now, I already knew which firms would come up high in the Google search results. I knew which IFA businesses were on top of their search engine optimisation game, but just because they were good at SEO, didn't necessarily mean that they were right for my mother-in-law. I wanted to see which of the websites that came up in the results actually 'spoke' to her.

Having not previously been particularly interested in the internet, she found the process intriguing and fun – but also frustrating.

We trawled through about fifteen websites and Beryl asked me to print them off.

This we did and then laid them out in piles on our kitchen table. For me it confirmed everything I had suspected, because Beryl struggled to find one that jumped out at her.

She made careful notes on a separate piece of paper, noting points such as apparent trustworthiness, location and qualifications – though whilst being impressed with the latter, they weren't really at the top of her priority list.

Between them all, they had pictures of older people walking hand in hand on beaches, laughing and playing with grandchildren and looking generally pleased with life.

At one point Beryl asked,

"I assume they don't work for free, but I can't see what they charge to work with someone like me…"

Then suddenly she stood back from the table pointing to one of the piles and announced,

"I like the look of him; where do I write to him?"

I took a closer look and noticed that she had chosen someone who was very highly qualified, but I could immediately see that there was much more to him than just qualifications and experience.

It was his *About Us* page that Beryl was pointing at, and it was completely different from all of the others.

Instead of the usual *"James Miller joined County Wealth Management in June 2009…"* etc., this one barely mentioned his business credentials.

In fact, it did quite the opposite, putting all of the focus on *why* he became a financial adviser, how it is a family business and that he works with his wife and daughter, his love for tennis, his passion for English Springer Spaniels, his list of favourite walking holiday routes in Spain, his top ten fiction books, music concerts that he has been to with his wife and his current 'Wine of-the-Month' recommendation.

At the time, Beryl was going through some family issues and the house move from the other end of the country had taken some toll on her. However, it seemed that this adviser's website was **speaking directly to her** and in a language that she could understand. And to be clear, she was far from being someone that you might describe as 'vulnerable'; she was (and still is) sharp, detailed, insightful and not naïve when it comes to matters of investment and personal finance.

In short, Beryl wanted an adviser who was on the same wavelength as her. She had read enough in the newspapers to know what standards were expected of an IFA in terms of professionalism, so that aspect of making the choice was a given.

So it was no surprise to me that her first words were *"I like the look of him…"*

"People buy people" as my Dad had told me many years earlier. Turns out that people buy people online, just as much as they do face to face.

So what has this got to do with video profiles?

Simple; the IFA that Beryl chose had **told a story** on his *About Us* page. In just a few paragraphs and a few photos of him with his family and Springer Spaniels and playing tennis, he had communicated in a very human way – one that is very hard to ignore.

An incredibly powerful way to tell a story is through video, and a new trend that is developing is to turn your *About Us* text into a video or even a short movie.

As biography writing expert Caroline Mays of Switchblade Lemonade says,

"Create a bio so good, you could make it a movie".

Take a look at Caroline's own profile video at https://vimeo.com/238678086 to see what I mean.

Yes, this will cost you a little more to put together, but something like *that*, will without a shadow of doubt make you stand out from the crowd.

And here's a prediction for you – it is only a matter of time until LinkedIn will give members the option of having a video profile alongside your current text profile. *That* will be a game changer for those who take up the option.

One consultant I know is taking video so seriously that he has removed all the text off his website and replaced it with a video and a contact box.

Are you ready to get started with video?

Pod Power

Podcasting

First, to set the scene, here are a few numbers from the website Podcast Insights for podcast consumption in the USA as at December 2019:

It is estimated that there are over 800,000 podcasts, with over 30 million individual episodes. Compare this to June 2018 when Apple confirmed that there were 550,000 podcasts

70% of the US population is familiar with the term "podcasting" – up from 64% in 2018 (Infinite Dial 19)

51% (144 million) of the US population has listened to a podcast – up from 44% in 2018 (Infinite Dial 19)

32% (90 million) listened to a podcast in the last month – up from 26% in 2018 (Infinite Dial 19)

22% (62 million) listen to podcasts weekly – up from 17% in 2018 (Infinite Dial 19)

16 million people in the US are "avid podcast fans" (Nielsen Q1 2018)

Podcast listeners listen to an average of 7 different shows per week, up from 5 in 2017

80% listen to all or most of each episode

Podcast listeners are much more active on every social media channel (94% are active on at least one – vs 81% for the entire population)

Podcast listeners are more likely to follow companies and brands on social media

Podcast listeners tend to be loyal, affluent and educated

Podcast listeners are more likely to subscribe to Netflix or Amazon Prime (meaning they are less likely to be exposed to TV advertising)

Podcast listeners are more likely to own a smart speaker (Amazon Alexa or Google Home)

I've mentioned podcasting a few times in this book, but let's have a closer look at why it works so well as a marketing tool for financial advisers.

And for this purpose I want to bring Pete Matthew back to the stage.

As I mentioned earlier, Pete's YouTube channel Meaningful Money sets the standard for an adviser's use of video to communicate personal finance education and concepts. His videos are simple but very effective.

But a few years ago I was chatting to him and we talked around the idea of podcasting. From my own research at the time, it seemed that marketing gurus around the world were beginning to think that podcasting was actually going to be bigger than video. That seemed unlikely, but whilst it has been known for years that audio on its own was remarkably influential in people's lives, it was the delivery mechanism that would make podcasting such a big deal for marketers and content creators.

What's more, as our lifestyles get busier and busier, and whilst technology gives us more and more ways to consume information, it became inevitable that podcasting was going to catch on in a big way. We can now listen in the gym, on a train, walking down the street, whilst out running, on a plane – podcasts can be consumed anywhere.

Firstly, why is audio so powerful?

My brother John makes radio commercials for a living. He is also a voiceover artist for radio and TV advertisements, as well as many service announcements in public places.

A number of airlines use his voice on their public address systems and apparently his is the last voice you hear when your plane is about to crash…

That golden nugget aside, John tells me that radio has a quality known as 'cut-through'. Although your favourite radio presenter often broadcasts to millions of people each week - to you in your kitchen, shower or car, it *feels* as though he or she is speaking directly to you. And that is cut-through, and one of the reasons why radio advertising is so effective.

John told me a while ago that when the advertisements come on when listening to commercial radio, something like 75% of us do not change channels, whereas when the ads appear on television, 75% of us do change channels or fast-forward.

Radio and audio also make our brains work harder when we are listening to it, and our imaginations fill in the blanks to the message or story being told, thus making it far more memorable. When I was younger, I always used to think that the idea of tennis, snooker or cricket on radio was a ridiculous idea, but now I realise that our minds create the visuals for us as we listen to the commentator.

In essence, a podcast is an audio file that we can listen to on a variety of devices. Think of it as a radio programme, but one that you play back on your phone. It becomes a podcast when listeners are able to subscribe to the recording so that it automatically appears on our playback device every time there is a new episode.

People normally find and subscribe to podcasts online, and the main podcast directories are:

- Apple Podcasts (iTunes)
- Google Play
- Spotify
- Stitcher
- Podchaser
- TuneIn

There are of course others, including directories for specific topics. Many podcast hosts also use Facebook, Twitter, YouTube and other social media platforms as distribution points.

There are various ways to get your podcast into these directories, but for the most part your audio file has to be hosted (stored) somewhere with an RSS (Really Simple Syndication) feed, from which the directories pull your content.

There is a little more to it than that, but it's easy to pick up once you get started. The host that I and many others use is called Libsyn, which you will find at https://libsyn.com. There is a small cost to hosting, but nothing that will put you off.

Libsyn also provides you with useful stats on the number of downloads, location of listeners, etc. This is really useful because you can see at a glance which episodes have been most popular and from there you can be guided on the best content to post for future recordings.

Now, to some numbers…

As at the end of September 2019, Pete has posted 399 podcast episodes, with total downloads just short of three million. And for a period of six weeks over August and September he had picked up twenty-five new client enquiries directly attributable to his podcast.

By any standard, three million downloads is incredible, and puts Pete's podcast in the big league. And you have to bear in mind that he isn't a 'celebrity' like a TV presenter, actor or traditional radio presenter. Pete is a financial planner in Cornwall – just like any other professional financial adviser anywhere in the UK or wider world.

What's more, the topic is personal finance – arguably not the sexiest of topics. When you consider that the most popular podcasts cover music, TV and movies, comedy, news, education, technology and kids and family, this really is a fantastic result.

Three million downloads strongly suggest that there is high demand for information on personal finance when presented by an expert.

The icing on the cake for Pete is that the enquiries that he is receiving as a direct result of the podcast, are as close as he can get to 'perfect'.

Pete is not the only financial adviser who hosts his own podcast, though in the UK you can currently count the number of them on the fingers of one hand. Clearly there is demand, so it's surprising how few advisers put one out.

We must also mention Catherine Morgan of The Money Panel again.

Her podcast *In Her Financial Shoes* is rapidly growing in popularity and has multiple five-star reviews on iTunes. These are typical of some of her testimonials:

"I absolutely love this podcast. I can't wait for each new episode I am currently binge listening all the previous ones as I only recently discovered this. I learn so much every episode and can't wait to start seeing the changes it makes to my life."

"Catherine gives clear, jargon free information that anyone can take steps to follow. Truly life changing."

"All I can say is Wow! I thought I was pretty money savvy, but already have a number of great tips that I am off to investigate further and put into action."

And this one:

"Catherine is a genius! She knows what I don't know and then teaches me. This podcast is essential for women. Who knew that a podcast about money could be so interesting."

And that is just a few of them.

Not only does Catherine have phenomenal reviews for her podcast, but it has grown her a loyal following, attracted leads and got the attention of brands who want to partner with her.

It is thought that Martin Bamford of Informed Choice created the UK's first ever personal finance podcast back in 2007. At the time podcasting was in its infancy in terms of the technology and involved a lot of manual technical work to get it out there. Martin's podcast ran for about eight episodes, but he brought it back in 2014 as Informed Choice Radio. In their own words:

Informed Choice Radio is the personal finance podcast all about achieving your financial goals and living a better life.

New episodes are published every Monday and Friday morning, featuring expert interviews and practical tips for making the most of your money.

You'll learn from best-selling authors, thought leaders and personal finance experts.

Your host for Informed Choice Radio is Martin Bamford; a Chartered Financial Planner, Fellow of the Personal Finance Society and personal finance author.

At the time of writing the Informed Choice podcast is well on its way to its five hundredth episode, so another big player.

Pete, Catherine and Martin also upload their podcasts to YouTube, again to give additional visibility and continuity across different platforms.

Structuring your Podcast show

When starting out with a podcast, many people struggle to come up with ideas for the actual content, but this is easier than you might think. The first thing to decide though is your format, as this will usually drive the content. If you have ever listened to a podcast, you will know that they come in a variety of formats, so here are some that work well:

- Interviews – either over Skype/Zoom or in-person
- Conversations and co-hosts
- Panels
- Solo presentations – like a monologue
- Educational
- True stories and case studies
- A mixture of one or more of the above

There are other formats, but which are not normally appropriate or relevant for personal finance related content. Whichever you opt for, it is best to play to your strengths. Some people will be very comfortable 'just talking' for a period of time whilst others thrive in an interview scenario.

Either way, plan them out several episodes in advance, and whilst the immediacy of quick and off-the-cuff editions can work well, in an ideal world you should do a couple of practice runs before putting anything live.

Once you have decided on your format and have planned several episodes in advance, it is advisable to record three to five episodes before putting the first one live, so that you have several up your sleeve. Because once you have started this journey, you want to try and keep going, and having episodes ready and in the can will save you a lot of time and stress later.

Looking for content ideas? As well as the excellent UK personal finance podcasts that are already out there, do some research by listening to the wealth of other money and lifestyle related broadcasts that are available, and you'll soon start coming up with some great ideas of your own. Again, take a look at the Answer the Public website for ideas, along with questions that are being asked on Quora.

Look at money related content that is being posted on LinkedIn too and make a note of topics that could form the basis of podcast episodes.

Try also to think in themes, where for a period of time you cover one topic, then another – and so on.

Tone and Branding

You will also need to think about the tone of your podcast. What do you want it to sound like?

Will it be serious, in-depth and academic, lighter and more fun or something else?

Think about your own company branding and produce something that broadly matches it. You should also think about who, in an ideal world you would like to be out there listening to your podcast and create a tone and style that they will warm to.

This also goes for the artistic branding. For your website and the podcast directories you will need to have some 'cover' artwork that is clear, easy to read and again which reflects your company branding. Get some ideas by looking through iTunes and other podcast directories. Yes, you can create the artwork yourself using a variety of free tools such as Canva, but better still have it done professionally using a site such as Fiverr or Upwork.

By now this might be starting to sound like hard work but believe me it is worth it. We will revisit the benefits in a moment. But once you have planned it out and got into the swing of it, like anything else in life you will find it easy – not to mention a lot of fun.

But if you want a simple, quick and easy way to get started, try the all-in-one free solution provided by Anchor – see https://anchor.fm

Anchor is an app that you download to any device and gets you up and running very quickly.

So a reminder of why all this is a good idea:

- People interested in personal finance learn from experts – like you

- Podcasting builds relationships with your audience and helps people to get to know you before committing themselves further

- Podcasting is a valuable early step on your value ladder

- Podcasting gives your business a 'personality' whilst marketing your brand

- Podcasting is growing massively in popularity and so is a powerful new route to market for you

- There is still a great deal of room for new entrants – particularly in the UK

- It is a great alternative if you are not yet comfortable with video

- Very inexpensive to produce

- Your podcast will drive traffic to your website

- Podcasts are portable – people can take your broadcast wherever they go

- Once you have done your planning, podcasts are easy to create

- Podcasts are highly engaging and easily accessible

- Podcasts help you to reach new audiences

- Your personal network of contacts expands in size and quality

- They improve your speaking and listening skills and build your confidence as a communicator

- You get unexpected invitations to appear on other people's podcasts, run workshops, provide coaching and to speak at events. And yes, you personally start to build a following

- Your podcast deepens relationships with existing clients and professional introducers

- Your podcasts can be repurposed into other marketing content and also make great PR

- And finally… they can generate new income streams in their own right when people want to sponsor your broadcasts

If you want to learn more about podcasting, along with tips and ideas for content – plus information on the technical side of things, you will find a never-ending stream of help and advice on YouTube.

Radio Ga Ga

Radio interviews

Early on in this book I mentioned Keith Churchouse, a financial planner in Guildford, Surrey who used to sponsor local roundabouts. Here's a reminder of what he said,

"We sponsored roundabouts for many years, which made a huge difference. Clients would hear me on the radio, see the name on a roundabout, then get in touch."

I love the apparent simplicity of this approach – two marketing tactics used together which have a powerful overall effect. Very often it is the combination that makes it work so well.

A great example of a financial planner who has put radio at the heart of his marketing is David Braithwaite, Managing Director of Citrus Financial Management in Kent. I asked him how radio had worked for him.

"I started out in radio over 20 years ago – I always wanted to do it but didn't know how to get "in".

There was an IFA who used to appear on BBC Radio Kent, and I enjoyed listening to him and how he helped callers and explaining things clearly. I went to listen in one day when I was driving to see a client and they announced no show as sadly he had died. Sad news, but I then called the station and said, *"I can do that for you"* and that's how it started.

It has opened loads of doors, as once you appear there and are a model guest, (know your stuff, not a prima donna, arrive early and polite), you get asked back. It opened doors for me for BBC TV and ITV TV, all the main BBC channels - Radio 2, 5 Live, Radio 4 etc, as word spread.

There have been many benefits; firstly massive credibility in your clients' eyes and the best PR that money probably cannot buy. But also, I have now met many BBC employees (presenters, producers, editors etc) and give financial advice to a huge amount of them, so I am now the trusted "go to" person for financial advice in the BBC.

I know their pensions, benefits etc inside and out, and now having been trained as a presenter, I get to also live and work in their world which is a very privileged position to be in and one I am eternally grateful for.

Above all – I love it. Radio especially over TV is a fantastic medium to connect with people as they are effectively inviting you into their world (car, while they are ironing, school run etc) to listen to you.

I am incredibly lucky and still to this day think "wow" when I am on air, and it makes Mum and Dad proud."

I won't flog this one to death, but if you are comfortable with the sound of your own voice and have expertise to share, then radio is obviously an option for you

– both as a regular guest or even going as far as having your own show.

Clearly, unless invited out of the blue to appear by a radio station, you will need to make some approaches. Those of you who paid attention to the earlier chapter on PR will know what I'm going to say next...

If you have been sending out regular press releases about your business, and that your local radio station was included on the distribution list, then you will already have a relationship with them and relevant producers. So making an approach to appear as a guest should be a little easier.

A good time to reach out to radio producers is after there have been big announcements or changes in various aspects of personal finance – perhaps as a result of the Budget or when you have the results of an interesting survey.

Turn this information into a letter, email or press release and offer yourself as a potential expert interviewee on the topic. This could be a short over the phone interview or as a guest as part of their regular programming.

Some additional suggestions include,

- Do your research and find out the name of the presenter and ideally the producer. Once you have found them, dig around on LinkedIn and social media channels to learn some interesting facts about them – particularly things you have in common

- Make sure that you address the programme host or producer by name in your communication

- Write a compelling headline and introduction that makes them curious to know more

- Make a suggestion of up to five main topics for discussion – i.e. make life easy for them

- If you have any, highlight any previous interview experience, including industry panels at conferences, podcast interviews or industry press interviews etc. because this will increase their confidence that you will be a good guest

- Offer to provide sample interview questions. Radio hosts may or may not use them, but it demonstrates professionalism to provide them. Come up with a list of up to a dozen questions that you think the listeners might like answers to

- Include a summary/biography and perhaps a link to your LinkedIn profile, website and any professional facing social media. Don't forget to stress that you are a local business to them

- Offer to promote the interview through your social media channels etc.

"Your Home may be at Risk…"

Radio advertising

U nlike being interviewed or having your own show, advertising on radio means having to get out your credit card. But not as much as you might think.

Radio advertising has an interesting set of benefits:

- Radio still has a higher reach than any other platform. According to one source, in the US alone over 92% of American adults listen to radio every week

- In the UK, 88% of the population tune in to radio every week, with 65% tuning into digital radio over the same period. There are over 300 commercial stations and a rapidly growing stream of digital outputs (Source RAJAR March 2019)

- Targeting can often be powerful because radio stations already target specific demographics and market segments

- People build relationships with their favourite presenters and stations, so your commercial messages are heard in an environment which feels homely, comfortable and trusted

- It is easy to be regular and consistent in your advertising on radio and so reach your audience repeatedly

- You can experiment (split test) across different time slots and days of the week

- With creativity, your advertisements can be highly memorable

- Radio advertising is one of the most cost-effective forms of advertising available

- Like podcasting, radio is portable. Your advertisements will go with your listeners

- New radio technology is being taken up in big numbers – for example Alexa devices and other smart speakers. Smart speakers give listeners the opportunity to respond instantly to your advertisement by asking for further information on brands, products and services

- Return on investment is easy to measure

- Remember what we said about cut-through... People rarely change channels and are loyal in a world where we proactively try to avoid commercials

If you want more facts and figures check out the RAJAR website at https://www.rajar.co.uk. In their own words "RAJAR is Radio Joint Audience Research and is the official body in charge of measuring radio audiences in the UK. It is jointly owned by the BBC and the Radiocentre on behalf of the commercial sector."

Many people feel that maybe radio is getting a bit old fashioned, but as you can see it has much going for it and will for many years to come. Simply make an approach to your local station(s) and see what they have to say.

And don't forget to think strategically in your marketing, by combining it with other initiatives that you are running.

~

There has been some recent good news that will be extremely helpful to financial advisers wanting to advertise on radio. In February 2020, it was announced that lengthy radio advertising terms and conditions in the UK and Europe are set to be a thing of the past as new guidelines will allow them to be more concise.

According to Radiocentre and the leading media magazine Campaign, the move aims to make it easier for listeners to absorb and recall key information.

In a Press Release, Radiocentre said that phrases that are not always required but often used include "subject to status", "over 18s only" and "you will not own the vehicle".

Radiocentre also said that some brands have been put off using radio because of the lengthy terms and conditions required. It estimates that terms and conditions cost the industry £120m a year through lost revenue, airtime costs and reduced return on investment.

What's more, this guidance has been approved by the Financial Conduct Authority, with Siobhan Kenny, chief executive of Radiocentre saying,

"Shorter, punchier terms and conditions are proven to be more effective as there is a greater chance listeners will recall the relevant and most important details at the right time. This new guidance will help advertisers get their message across in a way that is clear, fair and not misleading, and will simultaneously relieve the nation's ears by improving the radio listening experience."

Site for Sore Eyes

Your Website

One of the top three best potential sources of new leads is an adviser's website. Unfortunately, the overwhelming majority of financial advisers' sites simply are not doing their job.

They may *look* amazing; indeed the visual quality of many advisers' sites is fantastic – unfortunately they are not converting people who visit – even the *right* people who visit.

A financial adviser's website should, for the most part do one of three things:

1. Add value and services to *existing* clients, or
2. Convert ideal prospects/visitors into enquiries, or
3. Promote or sell something – like a course, seminar, book etc.

It should not try to do all three, for reasons that will become apparent.

A fourth option is to have a website that is designed only for viewing by your professional introducers.

Over the last two years I have been looking in detail at financial advisers' websites. When I talk to them about the performance of their sites, there are usually a few clues as to what is or is not happening straight off the bat. A few simple questions are usually enough to get to the bottom of things:

Question: *How many new referrals have you had over the last couple of months from XYZ professional introducer?*

Typical answer: *Three or four.*

Question: *How many new referrals have you had over the last couple of months from existing clients?*

Typical answer: *Three or four.*

Question: *How many leads came through your website last month?*

Answer: *None that I'm aware of. Maybe one...?*

Question: *How many people visited your website last month?*

Answer: *I don't have those figures to hand, so I don't know.*

Question: *Who has those numbers?*

Answer: *I think our website designer might have them.*

Question: *Do you have a summary of how many people visited your website over the last twelve months?*

Answer: *No, I don't.*

Question: *What can you tell me about the performance of your website?*

Answer: *Not much really.*

And so on...

I interviewed one hundred and twelve financial advisers in the UK about their website performance, and the vast majority of the conversations went much the same as this.

An accurate summary of the responses was,

"Yes, we have a website and we're quite proud of it. It's mostly an online brochure but it rarely produces any leads."

The next step was to get hold of the stats for each of the websites concerned, and this is what I discovered:

The average number of visitors per month across all one hundred and twelve websites was 197. As websites go for financial advisers, 197 visitors is not too bad at all.

The average bounce rate – that is the percentage of people who arrived on the site and left without looking at a second page was 54%. And that is the average – there were some with bounce rates of 87%

This means that more than half of their visitors were leaving pretty well straight away. It is generally felt that a bounce rate of 25% or lower is quite good for most professional services websites.

So this means that out of the 197 visitors, around half left immediately, but still leaving about 90 who go on to look further around the site.

Now let's imagine that out of those 90, half of those are recruiters, competitors and others who are looking around for other reasons, you are still left with 45 each month who could possibly be genuine prospects.

Before we go on to ask what happened to the remaining 45, let's look at some other stats that are crucial for a financial advice business to know:

- Number of site visitors each week, month, quarter etc.

- Bounce rate

- Number of pages viewed

- Which pages were viewed

- Time spent on the site

- Time spent on each page (tells us which were the most popular pages)

- Search terms used in Google and other search engines that steered people to your site

- Location of each visitor

- The page where they decided to leave

Tools such as Google Analytics provide a wealth of valuable data, most of which is not needed by financial advisers (unless you have a highly eCommerce focused website), so the list above will give you everything you need to know.

I also looked at the design of all the websites, and whilst for the most part they were professional and (sort of) informative, there were some other interesting observations.

- They all said the same thing

- They all had similar imagery, often featuring lighthouses, compasses, sailing boats and cruises, green shoots, attractive older people walking hand in hand along seafronts, grandparents flying kites with grandchildren, violins and musical instruments, ballooning trips and people sitting in deckchairs

- Hardly any offered a free 'special report' or download of value such an eGuide

- Multiple clickable links on the home page

Let's just explore that last one for a moment, because it's at the heart of why visitors are not converting into enquiries.

In fact, across the one hundred and twelve websites, the average number of clickable links on the home page alone was 34. Put it another way, that is 34 distractions or 34 calls to action.

This is a problem that is a hangover from when financial advisers first started having websites. Back in the day, the perceived wisdom was that the home page of your website needed to be 'sticky'. In other words, it needed to hold people there and not let them go.

If there was enough great value on the home page, the idea was that your visitor would be suitably impressed, convinced that you were an expert (as evidenced by all the content) and that you were bound to have the answers to their questions. All they needed to do was pick up the phone and talk to you. What's more, several providers offered plug-in tools and calculators for advisers' websites – further adding to the content and general clutter.

In the early days, that approach worked fine. Financial advisers who were early adopters of websites generally reported good levels of enquiries coming in as a direct result of their web presence. And bear in mind there were very few social media sites as we know them today to speak of.

Website design, style and aesthetics didn't seem to matter either back then – it was all about the content. Martin Bamford at Informed Choice was an early website adopter and was the first to admit that their website at the time was not exactly a thing of beauty, yet it did the job very well.

I was working for Permanent Insurance during the early days of advisers having websites, and we developed a plug-in whereby a visitor to an adviser's website could get a term assurance quote there and then. If the site visitor liked the look of the quote, they could download an application form, complete it by hand and then put it in the post to Permanent's head office.

The application would be underwritten, terms offered, and if the client went ahead, the adviser from whose site they had obtained the quote would pick up the commission – without having done a thing! I distinctly remember this as a key moment when many of the more forward-thinking advisers suddenly realised that the internet and websites were going to be a game changer.

This was around 2001, but whilst the look and feel of adviser websites has changed very much for the better, the strategy behind them hasn't. The strategy is still to pile in as much content as possible, with no thought whatsoever for how consumers actually use websites.

The fundamental difference between then and now is subtle but important.

In 2001 we were using the internet very much like a fancy Yellow Pages. Today we use it to self-educate *before* we use it as a directory, so when people arrive on our websites, they are very much better informed on a given topic than they were before.

For example, if you are a senior executive nearing retirement, your pension, income and future lifestyle will be very much on your radar. You will be consuming news, blogs and articles, watching videos and possibly listening to podcasts on the topic. Algorithms will know you are interested in the topic, so social media will feed you even more content and advertising that you are likely to find interesting.

In short, you will have a pretty good idea of what's what when it comes to pensions and lifestyle in retirement. Indeed, there is so much information available to you on the internet, you may even be minded to going down the DIY route (and that will increasingly happen). You might even question why you even need a financial adviser at all...

But there will still be many who, having self-diagnosed and thoroughly informed themselves on all matters pensions, will decide that the right thing to do is to visit an IFA to see what more they can add to your knowledge and very possibly to apply their expertise to your situation.   They will do one or more a number of things:

- Reach out to advisers whose podcasts they have listened to

- Attend a seminar being held by a local IFA

- Take advice or recommendations given by their company, colleagues or HR department

- Ask the opinion of a friend at their gym or in the pub

- Reach out to an IFA who has written a blog or article on the topic

- Look for IFAs or financial planners on LinkedIn

- Follow up advertisements and posts on Facebook

- Search for financial advisers who have posted videos on their YouTube channel

- Directly ask friends on Facebook or Twitter if anyone can recommend an adviser

- Search Google

- Use an adviser directory tool

- And more…

You have many choices as to how you find the right financial adviser for you. But one way or another, at some point you will look at some advisers' websites, and if on arrival they do not speak directly to you, your issues, your problems and your questions, or give you some immediate value, you are more than likely going to join the 54% of visitors who bounce off the website.

The problem with financial advisers' websites today is that they are too generic and do not engage with visitors in a way that sits well with how they use the internet. Most have already educated themselves to a greater or lesser degree on the personal finance matter they are concerned about, and now want a specialist who can add their skill, expertise and experience to the situation.

If all the visitor finds on your website is fluffy stuff like,

"Here at family-owned Jones & Co Financial Planning, we are committed to empowering you with knowledge, in order to help you fulfil your goals whilst ensuring you enjoy a comfortable retirement…",

…they will simply move on.

Couple this with multiple links on the home page (34 on average) that take you round the houses and link to topics that you are not interested in, it is no wonder that such sites do not convert perfectly good and often high-quality visitors/prospects. All these links succeed in doing is to confuse, and a confused mind will always say No.

If I'm looking for a pensions *expert* and I see on your site that you also offer mortgage advice, I might be tempted to think that you are not in fact a pensions expert but a jack of all trades. That may sound a little unfair, but I know that most advisers won't want to be giving such an impression. It might seem a natural thing to list out all of your services, but it doesn't impress visitors who are looking for specialists/experts.

Websites like this are no better than having your team hand out leaflets at the local shopping centre, in the vain hope that someone will be interested. For most people visiting your site, it is akin to walking into a brick wall.

What is the solution?

It starts with what we call ourselves – Financial Planner, Financial Life Planner, Financial Adviser, Independent Financial Adviser, Wealth Manager etc. *We* all know what it means, but in this day and age it's all a bit vague.

If I want a nose job, I don't just want a Surgeon, I want a Rhinoplasty *Specialist* such as a Consultant Surgeon specialising in Nasal Plastic Surgery or a Consultant ENT and Rhinoplasty Surgeon.

When I looked at those one hundred and twelve financial advisers' websites, the overwhelming majority did not suggest specialism in any one particular area, but just listed out that they offer advice on some or all of the following,

Pension planning

Retirement planning

Investment management

Savings

Cashflow planning

Financial reviews

Life assurance

Business protection

Inheritance tax planning

Mortgages

Equity release

Later life planning

Employee benefits

Wills and estate planning

And often even more.

Arguably the catch-all title of 'Financial Planner' might even be too vague for some people in this day and age. And I know that there are increasing numbers of advisers who are realising that the word 'advice' is more than a bit fuzzy and ambiguous.

We have suggested earlier that dominating a niche is one strategy, but even if you do not yet feel comfortable taking that route throughout your business, your website should suggest that you do specialise so that it immediately gets the attention of, say, the executive nearing retirement mentioned earlier.

You have some options and we will look closer at some of them:

1. Create a 'funnel' website for your *one* main area of specialism, or

2. Create a separate funnel site for *each* of the advice areas that you offer, or

3. Create a funnel site that covers all areas of advice that you offer, or

4. Dramatically reduce the number of clickable links on the home page of your current website, or

5. Analyse your current website and note in detail which pages of your site hold visitors on for the longest period of time – then model the copy and content onto the home page. I.e. repeat what appears to already be working elsewhere

For the avoidance of doubt, it is entirely possible to run a successful financial advice business *without* a website. A couple of high-profile financial planners have picked me up on this, so that is fair enough. But being realistic, even if you get referrals through a variety of sources or a regular flow of leads through seminars and workshops, most people will still want to check you out online before talking to you. So it is important that you have a website of some sort along the lines of one of the five models I've listed above.

I'm also aware of three or four IFA firms who don't have websites, but they use and promote their LinkedIn and Facebook pages as alternatives.

Remember, if your online presence is a promotional tool for your business, then the object of the exercise is to have a website that **converts the right visitors into people who make enquiries**. To do that, it needs to appeal directly to their main issues, questions and concerns. And that is exactly what a funnel website does.

Equally, if you have a LinkedIn profile or Facebook page as above, then again, the objective should be to convert the right visitors into enquiries. More on this later.

Funnels

If you are not familiar with the term, a funnel website is a very simple landing or home page. It focuses its content on one main task – getting the attention of your prime target market and encouraging them in a clear and deliberate way to take some sort of action.

If you are an adviser who specialises in pension planning for (say) consultant surgeons, then your landing page will ONLY address their needs. That and nothing else.

It goes without saying that if pension planning for consultant surgeons is your area of expertise, then by definition you will already be aware of what these needs are. You will know their tax issues, their frequently asked questions and other technical issues unique to this group.

The next feature of your funnel/landing page is to **prove** that you have this expertise, by offering some **immediate value** that will satisfy their curiosity. This is usually provided in the form of a free and instantly downloadable eGuide given in exchange for their email address. If you clearly appear to have the expertise they need and you are offering something that will add to their own knowledge, then giving you their email address is a fair exchange of value and one that most people are comfortable with. The moment they download the eGuide, they are now on the first step of your value ladder – and so the relationship begins.

The eGuide should be simple but high value, and often the most effective downloads will answer questions that you know they have. It can be in the form of a Special Report that you have written or even something like a Tips Guide that promises *"Twenty ways for consultant surgeons to increase their income in retirement."*

Other options to offer instead of an eGuide can include an educational video, audio recording, webinar or even a book, but usually an eBook or eGuide works best.

Arguably, we could now describe this website visitor as a client. Not a client in the traditional sense of someone who has been through your normal financial advice or planning service – but a new type of client. They have made a small commitment to engaging with you and in doing so have put a toe in the water and experienced some aspect of your expertise and service.

If not a client, this is now a lead or prospect – whatever you want to call them. They may even refer you to others, even at this early stage of the relationship.

In summary:

1. You attract the right people to your landing page/funnel

2. You offer them something free but high value which answers some of their key problems/questions

3. They give you their email address in exchange for your free download

4. You have a new prospect/client who you now follow up in the normal way, initially through email and then leading to the telephone and a meeting.

Remember – most financial advisers already have people visiting their websites each month, so they have leads right under their noses. But because their websites lack real focus on specific needs and issues, the visitors either leave, get confused or don't take any further action.

The funnel approach gives that focus whilst providing 'bait' that will attract the enquiries you really want.

But what if your financial advice business doesn't niche on consultant surgeons nearing retirement?

Maybe you have more focus than you think…

When I asked the one hundred and twelve financial advisers to describe a typical client, every single one of them was able to articulate a 'type' of client that they dealt with. Some were more vague than others in their description, but for the most part it was obvious that the adviser concerned had very real expertise on the financial planning needs of a clearly identifiable group of people. In some cases, the niche or focus was extremely clear to see.

When I then asked if they would like more clients like these, the answer was always *"Yes"*. So with a funnel approach, they could then go about focusing their landing page on the exact needs, questions and issues faced by that group of people.

Yes, it will always be very much easier if you focus on a tight niche like professional Bass fishermen, heart surgeons, CEOs of FTSE 100 firms, lawyers who want to retire early, first-time buyers etc., but most financial advice firms can identify, if not a niche, but groups of specific types of people.

You then create a funnel aimed at them, complete with a lead magnet such as an eGuide, eBook, Tips Sheet etc.

How do I attract the right people to my website?

Bear in mind that you already have people on the books who either fall into your niche or a discrete client type. How did you acquire those clients?

You should already be keeping detailed notes on how your existing clients came to work with you. If you do, you will see that there are patterns – maybe they all came through referrals or a particular professional introducer. Maybe you have been running seminars or perhaps your clients are people you play tennis with. This book is highlighting multiple different ways that you can attract new clients, and some of the ideas will appeal to you more than others because each advice firm is different.

In short, do more of what you are already doing that works, but making allowance for new marketing tactics that you feel will be appropriate in your own market.

But the point about this chapter is that you are almost certainly missing out on attracting more of the clients that you really want, because your website is letting you down. **Your ideal clients are already visiting your website**, but as we saw from my research, the one hundred and twelve websites we looked at:

- Lacked focus
- Lacked differentiation
- Had far too many distracting links
- Did not offer immediate value through downloadable content
- Did not 'speak' directly to their target market

…so these site visitors left to go and do their own thing, or to re-think how they go about getting advice or perhaps went to another adviser that a friend recommended in the first place.

What's more, the financial advisers themselves had no idea this was happening because they didn't have a grip on their website numbers.

Here is my suggestion as to what to do next:

1. Get to know your current website by analysing your numbers and look at them every week from now on.

    Either ask your website person to get you the numbers or do it yourself. If Google Analytics is a bit overwhelming, an excellent tool that just gives you the basics is Clicky. Here's my link: http://bit.ly/clicky-calvert - it is free for the basic stats, though when you upgrade you can a lot of additional features, such as heatmaps which show where people click on your web pages.

2. Examine your website stats for three months before making any major changes, so that you have got a handle on the essential numbers – in particular the bounce rate. If it is under 25% that's a good place to be.

    If it is higher than 30% you can make improvements. If it is 50% or higher, you should make immediate changes to your home page along the lines that I have described, in particular get real focus, eliminate clutter, cut out all the links and offer a free download aimed at your ideal clients.

3. Gradually move to the funnel model, using tools such as ClickFunnels, Leadpages, Builderall, Kartra, Unbounce, Infusionsoft by Keap etc. There are also special landing page plug-ins for sites created on WordPress and the like.

    I use ClickFunnels and just love it. For one

monthly fee I can create multiple funnels/landing pages for multiple products and services – so when you cringed earlier at the idea of having a funnel for *each* of the services you offer, this is the solution. You pay once but can create multiple sites using the software.

What's more, once you have got the hang of the software (it is literally drag and drop), you can create a page in seconds, if not a few minutes.

When you use my ClickFunnels link, you can get a free trial at http://bit.ly/Philfreetrial2020

4. As you get more advanced, you should then start 'split-testing' your funnels, which means putting up different versions of your pages with different colours, wording and designs, so that you can see which works best in terms of conversions.

Often you will find that by changing words here and there, you can dramatically increase the number of conversions. So there is an element of trial and error, but that is the point – keep testing things until you optimise the performance of your page/site.

ClickFunnels provides this split-testing facility, though I'm sure some of the other landing pages software do too.

5. Start learning more about the art and science of copywriting. Whilst you might think that the wording on your site is down to your designer or

others in your firm, copywriting is a fantastic skill to have and will help you in many other facets of your life and business.

Quite simply, the words that you use on your website (funnel or otherwise) can make all the difference between attracting leads or turning them away. When you marry up the right website model (funnels) with the right wording, then you have something very powerful.

Remember the book I mentioned earlier? *Copywriting Secrets* by Jim Edwards – get yours at https://amzn.to/36DQGcs

Exceptions to the Rule

Exception #1

There is another type of website which can attract more of the right type of clients, which is the exact opposite of a funnel - and that is a blog.

We have mentioned blogging several times in this book, but in this instance I am suggesting that you could use it instead of, or as part of your website.

Instead of…

If you don't want to have a funnel or a traditional brochure website that doesn't perform, you could instead put all your efforts into a blog.

However for this to attract enquiries it needs to be regular and consistent. The purists will tell you that you need to blog every day, if not once a week minimum.

Once a week is very doable once you get your head round it, with the occasional extra one as the mood takes you.

Your blog has three functions:

- Regular, consistent and ongoing proof of your expertise and value

- The ability to focus your content on a niche or discrete group

- Increasing your visibility in Google search results

With a blog there is no need to include multiple links as on a traditional website – all you need is a box or space for people to contact you.

And a quick technical point, your blog should have an RSS feed so that people can subscribe to it (the same as for your podcast that we mentioned earlier).

Your blog will be on a site all on its own, using for example WordPress, Blogger, Wix, Medium and others.

In summary, instead of a traditional website or funnel, you just focus on giving value through your blog.

As part of…

If you really don't want to go down the funnel route, then I would strongly suggest bringing your current site to life by adding a blog to it.

'Bringing your site to life' is important because most financial adviser brochure websites never change from one week to the next. When you add a blog to it and regularly add new posts, the visitor gets the sense that your business is alive, kicking and has something to say. That in itself will attract a few more enquiries – particularly if the content of the blog is aimed at the needs, issues and questions of your ideal site visitors.

Exception #2

Another exception to the rule is to add video testimonials. If you must have a brochure site, then put the emphasis on your video testimonials. Remove as much content and clutter as you can and put the testimonials up front and centre.

With this in mind, it is worth re-reading the earlier chapter on video testimonials.

Exception #3

Again, if you want to keep your brochure site, I strongly recommend dramatically enhancing the About Us page so that it really goes to town on the personal and people side of the business.

Please re-read the chapter on Video Profiles and the story about how my mother-in-law Beryl chose her financial adviser.

Again, strip away as much clutter as possible and focus on the *people buy people* concept.

The Future

This has been quite a lengthy chapter but one that I hope strikes a chord with you. What I have described is the new but proven way to attract and convert more of the enquiries you really want.

Website design (look, feel and user interface) will inevitably evolve as tastes change, but the fundamental principle of successful sites will remain – that of laser focused copywriting that leads to an offer of immediate value which answers the problems, questions and issues of your ideal clients.

The ever-popular themes of compasses, lighthouses and attractive grandparents flying kites on sunny beeches with grandchildren may *look* attractive on financial advisers' websites, but just don't cut it any longer.

To revisit the medical analogy, if I was a senior consultant heart surgeon nearing retirement, and someone who wants to ensure that I have my pension ducks in a row, through one route or another I may well find my way to a financial planner's website.

If that financial planner's site speaks directly to the issues that I have identified through my own reading and research, and appears to offer me a free, instantly downloadable guide that answers some more of my key questions - and from the perspective of an expert in pension planning for heart surgeons - it is extremely unlikely that I will not share my email address with that adviser.

If all I see is pictures of grandparents flying kites and waffle about *"... empowering me with knowledge, in order to help me fulfil my goals whilst ensuring I enjoy a comfortable retirement..."* – then sorry, I'm out of there.

Your website has the potential to be at the forefront of lead generation for your financial advice business, but whilst it functions as little more than a brochure, it will not perform. If you want it to start converting more of its visitors, you need to make it work much harder for you – and that will involve stripping it back, but adding in content which takes your ideal clients by the hand and leads them straight to your office door.

Quick observations

There are of course other exceptions to rules. During the course of writing this book, I've occasionally unearthed examples of adviser websites which perform extremely well. One financial planner mentioned that she was *"inundated with leads from her website"* with a couple of others making similar comments. I looked closer at their websites and noticed a few things:

- They are often very simple with no fuss.

- They often use the American spelling of Advisor with an 'o'. This is important because more people in the UK use the American spelling when searching

- They made a point of highlighting that client meetings can take place online using Skype/Zoom and secure communications.

- They have a pop-up message box inviting visitors to chat with them.

- They offer clear choices of service, including very inexpensive guidance, self-service and full planning. They also highlight training on how to use their own personal finance portal.

- They use simple and straightforward language without 'dressing up fluff'.

- There are very few clickable links on the home page, and those there are, predominantly are contact points (click to call, click to email, click to chat, click to send us message).

- Relaxed and friendly photos of their advisers were featured on the home page, with no lighthouses, compasses or smiling grandparents.

- And finally, they feature a client video testimonial.

In short, whilst these sites are not funnels, they are very engaging in that they draw you in quickly and make you want to engage with them.

Would you like a free appraisal of your website?
Get in touch at philip@financialadvice.marketing

Climbing the Ladder

Your Value Ladder

L et's now look closer at a concept I referred to in the previous chapter, and how it can dramatically enhance the effectiveness of your marketing - in particular the sentence,

"The moment they download the eGuide, they are now on the first step of your value ladder – and so the relationship begins."

We expect a lot from our clients and prospects. We put up a brochure-style website and we expect (or at least hope) that after reading our carefully crafted prose, they will decide that we are the financial adviser for them and will pay our fees.

In an internet era where our websites all say the same thing and where sophisticated consumers can self-educate on every aspect of personal finance and financial planning, we are expecting them to have a gut feel that one firm of advisers is more appropriate for them to contact than another.

It's a big ask.

So how do we encourage one person to decide to talk to us rather than the financial advisers next door?

One way is to follow the model that my mother-in-law Beryl was attracted to – that of emphasising the human touch. Another is what we covered in the last chapter – ensuring that the content on the home page of our website has laser focus on the needs, questions and issues faced by our ideal clients.

To do the latter requires the building of a value ladder.

In essence, a value ladder is a way to build relationships with prospects so that they can get to know us, get to understand our expertise, build the relationship and establish trust – so that purchasing our highest value services becomes a logical thing to do in due course.

In the earlier example, the downloading of our eGuide is the first step on our value ladder. It is an easy and logical step to take on the part of the prospect because he or she gets instant value in exchange for their email address – a low risk step for them to take.

Let's look at an example from another professional service provider such as a dentist.

Value Ladder for a Dentist

If we are looking for a new dentist, from the outside, one dental practice often looks much the same as another, so how do we choose who to put our trust in?

Maybe we are looking for some teeth straightening or expensive cosmetic work, and clearly if we are going to be getting out our credit card, we are going to need to be able to trust the professional concerned.

Written testimonials on the practice website will be helpful, but they only go so far. A personal recommendation will be useful, but what if we don't know someone who has had cosmetic work done at this particular dentist? What we would rather see are video testimonials from real patients.

In an ideal world, though not always possible, we would also like to be able to try before we buy. One way for us to do that is to experience some of the practice's lower value services first – such as teeth cleaning or whitening, or even a check-up.

That way we can get a feel for the place and its people and then start to make a judgement based on our **personal** experience.

The value ladder approach is becoming increasingly popular amongst dental practices. Its sole purpose is to:

- Get you in the building
- Treat you like a king or queen
- Give you some real value for free

You will often now see dental practices offering free teeth cleaning or even free whitening just to give you the opportunity to experience their service. Of course there was a time when teeth whitening was something only celebrities could afford, and although it is now easily available to anyone, it is still perceived to be a high value service.

Even better for the dental practice is that some free services are not even performed by the dentist. Either way, the free services are the bait to get you in to try before you buy. Once there, they make a big fuss of you and some even ask for a video testimonial while you are in the building.

It goes without saying that while you are enjoying your free teeth cleaning, the hygienist or whoever is performing the treatment may highlight any other work that they feel you need. If you have enjoyed the whole experience, then it becomes very much more likely that you will come again in due course, and this time more than happy to get out your credit card. Some months down the line, once your confidence and the relationship has grown, you will be more inclined to get that cosmetic work done that you have been thinking about.

You see the same value ladder approach being offered at gyms and health clubs where they offer you free membership for a period of time. Their goal is to get you in the building and to experience the amazing service and facilities. Later, after you are a paid-up member, they will be looking to offer you more services which gradually increase in value.

A chiropractor might also have a value ladder, where over time you are offered the following services:

Consultation > Massage > Acupuncture > Personalised workout > Ongoing care plan > Wellness retreat

As you can see, the value of the services increases with time.

How about my own value ladder for IFAs?

In an ideal world, I would offer on my website my Premium Weekend Marketing Retreat. This is held at an upmarket country hotel, and after welcome drinks and a high-quality dinner, we take a deep dive into marketing for financial advice businesses.

The weekend also includes entertainment, including presentations by some speakers who are experts in their field.

It comes with a four-figure price tag, but to require a financial adviser to find it on my website and expect them to pay for it without having met me or experienced any lower price services first, is unrealistic.

So I adopt the value ladder approach which includes some or all of the following.

At the bottom of the ladder is free membership of LifeTalk – my online community for financial advisers. There they can network with other advisers, share best practice, exchange ideas, get answers to their business questions – and so on. Several IFAs have suggested that I should charge for membership, such is the value within it, but I currently give free access as a way of giving them a great experience right at the beginning of their relationship with me.

After they join the group/forum, my value ladder progresses:

Free eBook or eGuide > Book(s) & Audio books > Free or low-cost webinar > Live, chargeable workshop > Full day masterclass > Three online coaching calls > In-house training > Twelve month one-to-one coaching programme > Weekend marketing retreat

It is not 'compulsory' for everyone to follow the process in order; some people will read one of my books or watch a webinar and straight away ask if I can come in and train their team for the day. Through this pre-planned approach, what I am really trying to do is to give myself the best possible chance that people will gradually progress up the ladder one way or another.

It is also possible to upsell people from one step to something else, particularly where it would seem a logical step to take. For example, I might give away an eBook for free, but simultaneously offer them the audio version for (say) £15. If they have already committed to downloading the eBook, it dramatically increases the likelihood that they will pay for the audio book version.

This approach is all about helping clients to take small steps forward in the relationship with you, so that they feel comfortable ascending your value ladder and progressing towards the point where they purchase your highest value service.

What about the Value Ladder for Financial Advisers?

Having read the examples above, you can now begin to see how through a pre-planned value ladder of your own, you can take someone who found your website and progress the relationship with them in a way that will feel comfortable and natural.

Here is a potential value ladder for a financial adviser. It goes without saying that you are not going to include absolutely everything in this list, but almost all advisers could use some of the products/services listed to create a simple ladder of three, maybe four steps that would easily work for them.

Free eGuide > free eTips sheet > eBook > Book > Audio book > Podcast > Educational videos >

Thirty-day challenge > Webinar > Online course > Seminar > Online community > Your own networking events > Mastermind meetings > Financial Planning > Inner circle membership > Weekend or overseas retreat

So a real version might be:

Free eGuide > Seminar > Financial Planning

Or perhaps:

Free eTips sheet > Educational videos > Financial Planning

The trick to making this work, is to create a value ladder of products and services that meet the needs of your target market. Those products and services should highlight your knowledge, skills and expertise around the problems, issues and questions that they want answered.

I firmly believe that the value ladder approach is the future for financial adviser marketing – a gradual but natural process to build trust, build relationships and help clients to feel that a full financial planning relationship is the obvious way to go.

The unexpected side benefit of this approach is that as the value of your products and service increase, you can create new income streams along the way.

I have several examples of financial advisers around the world who initially included seminars as a marketing tool, but who quickly realised that they have real value, and so started charging for attendance. As is common when advisers host seminars, they attract new enquiries, but the attendees had essentially paid to be prospects. Most advisers who offer chargeable seminars part way along their value ladder quickly appreciate that seminars and events can produce a substantial new income stream – so you are able to make money from clients long before you ever provide your normal financial planning service.

Read all about it!

Newspaper Columns and Articles
in specialist magazines

L et's revisit some old-school marketing which is still very effective – and particularly valuable to financial advice firms.

One way to write an article is to post it as a blog on your website, LinkedIn or other platform of your choice. But long before the internet came along, businesses queued up to have their own column in their local or county newspaper. Even better if you could get a national column.

Whilst writing an article or articles in a local newspaper may feel a bit old-fashioned these days, they can still be very effective. Here's why:

- Your articles and column position you as an expert – if not *the* expert locally. It gives you credibility and validation.

- In addition to being seen as an expert on your topic, a regular column is great for your branding and local recognition.

- Your column supports and complements your other marketing.

- Despite easy access to the internet, a great many people still read or at least flick through one newspaper each week, so there are still a lot of eyeballs on local news.

- Writing articles for newspapers is essentially free marketing. And the fact that you are the person who has the column suggests that you have been officially endorsed by the paper.

- Writing regularly for a column gets you into the habit of creating steady and consistent content – and to a deadline. This is a great way to build a habit, making it much more likely that you will post regular blogs.

- Over time, you will find it easier to write quickly – and the quality of your writing improves too.

- Whilst some newspapers will request exclusivity for your article, there are always ways to repackage and repurpose your content for other marketing activities – such as videos, blogs, podcasts, webinars, online Q&A sessions and even tweets.

- A series of articles over several months can form the basis of a book.

- You can promote your column on your website, LinkedIn and in other social media profiles, again enhancing the perception of your expertise and credibility.

- And the icing on the cake – some newspapers may even pay you…

While you are slaving over a hot keyboard, don't forget that you can take the same approach with specialist magazines.

Quite often when I have been speaking at an industry or association conference, the organiser has approached me to write something for the in-house magazine as part of my fee. More often than not I will offer to write something anyway as part of my pitch to speak and usually it is accepted.

If you have several clients in a niche market, ask them what professional or industry magazines they read and approach the editors to see if they have any opportunities. Often you will find that they will accept a one-off article, and if they like your tone and style they may offer you a column for a limited period.

Don't forget, as for newspapers, many magazines also have an online presence, so your content on paper will probably end up online as well – and that's great for your search engine visibility too.

Whilst magazines come and go, there are still regular and popular publications in a wide variety of different industries – some of which may be representative of your client bank, including,

Accountancy

Agriculture

Automotive

Avionics

Business & Financial

Construction

Fashion

Healthcare

Horticulture

Hospitality

Human Resources

Internet

Legal

Manufacturing

Marine

Media

Oil & Gas

Outdoor Pursuits

Property

Retail

Services

Sport

Telecommunications

Textiles

Transport & Logistics

Travel

It can be a bit hiss and miss making your approach to editors but writing in industry publications and magazines can prove very fruitful over time. Don't expect to see your article in print and for the phone to immediately start ringing – sometimes it can be months later when people get in touch.

Just to throw a curve ball here and to revisit podcasts; when I have been a guest on someone else's podcast, it is often many weeks, if not months after the broadcast first went out when people make contact out of the blue, with the email usually beginning,

"Philip you won't know me, but I heard you on the XYZ podcast and wanted to get in touch."

It is often the same after you have written articles for newspapers and magazines.

Press is More

#JournoRequest

As well as approaching newspapers and magazines yourself, you can also wait for them to come to you.

You will remember from the PR chapter earlier how important it is to build relationships with local (and national) journalists, so that when there is news on a particular topic in which you have expertise, it increases the likelihood that they will come to you for comment.

There are a number of news services to which experts and financial advisers can subscribe to get on the radar of journalists and editors, but a really simple and effective way is to use Twitter. Journalists have a number of ways of finding experts to talk to, but Twitter has become very important in their work.

One way to find journalists who are requesting comment and stories is to follow the #JournoRequest hashtag. Journalists use this multiple times each day, and from time to time they are looking for expert comment on matters relating to personal finance.

Note that the hashtag is also used on LinkedIn and some journalists use #JournoRequests instead of #JournoRequest. Another one that is regularly used is #PRrequest.

I have also occasionally seen #JournoRequest being used by professional service providers on Instagram, where they highlight themselves as an expert in a given area.

In addition to comments, this hashtag is also used to find people willing to write articles and stories. Only today I saw these requests:

Calling all experts... Today I'm refreshing the specialists list for BBC South East. Can you give us expert insight on stories from psychology, to business, building, religion, arts, farming, personal finance, music?

And this:

A wealth management reporter would like to hear from #financialadvisors who seek clients w/wealth locked up in vested shares to provide insight on the #fintech platforms they guide such clients to, and the benefits seen.

And this one:

I'm writing a piece for a monthly publication and looking to speak to financial advisers who have experience of helping executives who have received large redundancy payments #journorequest

A useful tip when searching Twitter for journalists who are making requests, is to combine the #JournoRequest hashtag with one of your keywords, so for example when you include the word Pension this comes up:

*Looking for a female financial adviser to chat about using your **pension** (or pension-led funding) for a business. Please DM me #journorequest*

And here's another:

*#JournoRequest any IFAs that specialise in NHS **pensions**/annual allowance/LTA & are happy to chat, please get in touch*

And an example of one that includes the word Investments:

*Financial advisers, have you ever had a client consult you after coming across ads for **investments** promising high returns? Please get in touch #JournoRequest*

Simply search and follow the hashtag and dip in and out periodically to see if there is anything you can help with. Don't expect to see an avalanche of personal finance or financial planning related requests, but with patience you will occasionally find some golden nuggets.

There is also a website at https://www.responsesource.com which sends out daily summaries of such requests and you might also want to look at PressPlugs which matches journalists with experts at https://pressplugs.co.uk

Another site that journalists use to find experts is Expert Sources at www.expertsources.co.uk. There is a fee to join, but I have found it to be invaluable over the years.

In summary, providing comment for journalists in this way is free marketing, and it works. Some readers may recall the Unbiased Media 'Blue book' which before it was withdrawn, provided ample opportunities for advisers to engage with journalists.

Despite the loss of the Blue book, many financial advice businesses still put journalist engagement right at the centre of their marketing strategy because it has consistently been proven to be a powerful way to raise your profile in the press and online.

"Alexa, what day is it today?"

Voice Services

Earlier we looked at Podcasting, in particular the success of Pete Matthew with his Meaningful Money content.

Let's now look at something new, which many commentators believe will become the next 'big thing'. As to whether it will or not is another matter, but given the rapid growth in the use of Amazon Echo, Google Home and other internet enabled home devices, it is clear that there is an opportunity for some advisers to get on board while there appears to be plenty of potential.

As at the end of November 2018, according to Statista, 18.3% of UK homes with internet access had a smart speaker (over 20% in the US) which equates to 9.5 million active monthly users. This is almost double the previous year. Figures for 2019 are not yet available but all the predictions point to a further increase in usage.

Search

Some argue that it is still early days for smart speakers, but a key area of growth is how we use these tools, with search being at the top of the list. Here are some interesting figures compiled by Quoracreative:

- By 2020, 50% of all searches across the internet will be voice-based

- By 2020, 30% of all searches will be done using a device without a screen

- In the US, home adoption of smart speakers is predicted to rise to 55% by 2022

- Voice search queries are longer than regular text-based searches and tend to be three to five keywords in length

- 40% of adults now use mobile voice search at least once daily

- 20% of the searches on a mobile device are voice-based

- 25% of the queries on Android devices are voice-based

- 60% of smartphone users had tried voice search at least once in the past 12 months

- 55% of teenagers are using voice search on a daily basis

- Voice-based searches using a mobile phone are 3 times more likely to be location-specific

- People communicate with voice-activated speakers as if they were talking to a human, using courtesy words like "please," and "thank you," and even "sorry."

- 62% of those who regularly use their voice-activated speakers are likely to buy something through the device

- 58% of regular users, manage shopping lists on a weekly basis, using their voice-activated speakers

- 44% of regular users order groceries and other items using their voice-activated speaker on a weekly basis

- 52% of voice-activated speaker owners are open to information about promotions and deals

- 48% of voice-activated speaker owners are open to personalized tips and information

- 42% of voice-activated speaker owners are open to upcoming events or activities

- 53% of people who own a voice-activated speaker had a natural feeling while speaking with it

- More than half of people 55+ using a voice-activated speaker think it empowers them

It is worth pointing out that search results are not always 100% accurate, but the main manufacturers are working hard to improve this. That said, when searchers don't immediately find the answers they are looking for, they will often rephrase it until they get a result.

The implications for financial advisers are more technical than anything else. For example, the language we use when using voice search is different from when using text/web search. Voice search tends to be more conversational while text search is shorter and more to the point.

As use of voice search continues to grow, financial advisers will need to learn how to optimise their online presence for SEO (search engine optimisation) purposes. So this also has implications for the content we post online in that we will need to consider writing in a more conversational but concise tone.

For example long-tail keywords will become more important. 'IFA in Guildford' would be a short keyword, with 'IFA with pensions expertise in Guildford' being the long-tail version. A searcher might even say *"Where can I find an IFA in Guildford with pensions expertise?"* In other words it is much more specific and more likely to be used in voice search.

So when creating content on your website or blog that you want to be found for, you should ask yourself *how would someone find this if they were speaking instead of typing? How would they say it differently from when they were typing it?*

Skills

Another opportunity for the early adopting financial adviser is the Alexa Skills that can be created for use with Amazon Echo devices. For Skills, read Apps.

At its simplest, I can say to my Echo device, *"Alexa, play Planet Rock Radio"* and it will open almost immediately.

Whilst large brands have their own Skills, anyone can create their own with relative ease, and there is one particular type of Skill which can work well for financial advisers, and this is the Alexa Flash Briefing.

Flash Briefings are very short, informative pieces of pre-recorded audio – like news. Usually about a minute long, they are akin to a mini podcast and enable Alexa users to receive all the news they really want to hear quickly and easily.

In Amazon's own words:

You can create a flash briefing skill to provide Alexa customers with news headlines and other short content. Typically a flash briefing becomes a part of a customer's daily routine.

Customers get their flash briefing by asking their Alexa-enabled device things like:

"Alexa, give me my flash briefing" or "Alexa, tell me the news".

I have experimented with creating my own Flash Briefing and found it incredibly easy to do. If I can do it, anyone can, and no technical skills are required. To get started go to this link to learn more:

https://developer.amazon.com/en-GB/docs/alexa/flashbriefing/steps-to-create-a-flash-briefing-skill.html

I would also recommend searching YouTube for information on how to create Flash Briefings as there are plenty of helpful videos on the subject.

The marketing point though is that here is a new way to get your professionalism, expertise and credibility out there and **directly into people's homes** - and in a way that becomes part of their daily lives. So for the early adopters amongst you, this is an exciting opportunity.

And once you have the technical side of your Flash Briefing set up, your briefings are quick and easy to produce. As per Podcasts, it is advisable to record several episodes in advance, so that they can be queued up for automatic release on a daily basis within the Amazon system.

Quickfire and Fun Marketing Ideas

B efore we get into a couple more big marketing opportunities, here are some quick ones that you may want to consider as part of your mix.

Great with an ice cream - Theatre programme advertising

Earlier on we mentioned sponsoring local arts and cultural events. Your sponsorship will often include free advertising within the event programme, but don't forget advertising in its own right. Your local theatre, arts or cultural centre will be able to give you details.

A key point though, is that many financial advisers' key target demographic often goes to the theatre, so while they are waiting for the show to start, they can take a look at your advertisement. And don't forget the panto season when large numbers of families will see your advertisements over a period of several weeks.

Remember that earlier we talked about QR codes? When advertising in a theatre programme, remember to include a QR code, which when scanned plays a video message or even video client testimonials.

"… James Bond" - Cinema advertising

If you are thinking of advertising in theatre programmes, how about spreading your wings further and advertising in and around cinemas, including local billboards. Some key facts from cinema advertising experts DCM:

- 77% of the UK population are cinema goers

- Approximately 3.4 million people go to the cinema each week

- 87% of the audience are already seated before the ads begin

Plus:

- 58% of audiences are ABC1 demographic

- 51% are female

- 49% are male

Source: TGI Q4 2019. CAA Film Monitor Coverage & Frequency Data.

Audiences are also used to finance related advertisements, as the financial industry is the third highest spender on cinema advertisements.

Clearly the cost of cinema advertising can be high, particularly if you are a big brand, but cinema has its place for small businesses too as packages can be tailored to your requirements around specific films and locations. The good news is that audiences can be large and local; what's more they are for the most part totally focused on the screen and your ad will be watched without distraction.

Producing a cinema advertisement can be surprisingly low cost. Pearl & Dean offer 'DigiAds for as little as £95 per week and are specifically aimed at small local businesses.

"All we need is some high-resolution pictures and a suitable script and our in-house team can then create your very own DigiAd."

Sticky Business - Cars, Bumper Stickers and Wheel Covers

Remember Keith Churchouse from earlier who advertised on roundabouts? Let's keep the automotive theme going and go back to pre-internet days when anything and anything that moved could potentially host an advertisement.

Only, thanks to the internet, it is now easier than ever to find people who will carry an advertisement for your business on the side of their car. For example Car Quids and StickerRide are businesses that match up businesses with car owners who are happy to carry your advertisement – for a fee obviously.

The key part is that your advertisement doesn't end up on any old car, the platforms offering this service aim to match your advertisement up with the right type of vehicles and people.

The benefits are obvious, not least of which are that your advertisements will be seen multiple times in the area(s) of your choice.

Personalised 4x4 spare wheel covers are another great way for you to promote your local business, and I've seen multiple financial advice firms doing this over the years. The cost is ridiculously low too – often around £100 or £125 to include creation of your wheel cover artwork.

A Mug is for Life - Promotional Merchandise

A friend of mine is Director General of the British Promotional Merchandise Association (BPMA) and a few years ago he asked me to speak at their annual conference.

Having come from a provider background, I was very familiar with how large brands used promotional merchandising as part of their marketing, and doubtless readers of this book have in the past been recipients of providers' generosity in this area. The famous UNUM diaries, Zurich golf balls and the legendary L&G umbrellas to name a few.

Indeed, many financial advisers of old would give these gifts to their clients, because before digital printing came along, promotional merchandising was outside the budget of most advice firms.

But when I attended the BPMA conference, my eyes were opened to what is now possible in terms of 'merch' as it's known.

The benefits are clear and simple:

- Builds brand recognition
- Regular brand visibility
- Fun but valuable
- Inexpensive to produce

- Ideal way to say Thank You
- Great tools for giveaways at seminars, events, competitions and on social media
- Promotional gifts are also passed around, extending your reach

And you don't have to give away your merchandise – you can keep it for yourself! I have often seen financial advisers wearing their own running shirts and tee-shirts at local Park Runs and other outside events, or using their own branded coffee mugs in videos etc.

Again, this is a really simple marketing tactic, but well worth incorporating within your marketing mix.

Love local - Advertisements in local Magazines and Newspapers

There's not too much to say about this other than it is still a viable option for many financial advice businesses – particularly if local clients are important to you. Clearly, it is an alternative to advertising in theatre programmes as mentioned earlier.

Classified advertisements and other promotional content work particularly well when used in conjunction with something else that you are doing. For example if you have a column or an article in a publication, then complement it with an advertisement. If you have had a stand at your local fete, book an advertisement for the edition that carries a report and photos on the event.

Newspaper advertisements are also effective for promoting seminars and events. You will remember I mentioned IFA Andrew Brown who used seminars at the heart of his marketing. To get bums on seats he would often use local newspaper advertising, and through trial and error discovered what worked and didn't work in the copywriting. This trial and error also extended to the size and position of the advertisement in the paper, and for him an 'early right' (page 1, 3 and occasionally 5) worked best.

But here's the good news – the cost of advertising in newspapers and magazines has plummeted in recent years. In some specialist publications it has held up, but for general newspaper advertising you can pick up some amazing advertising deals. My friend Nick is a newspaper and magazine advertising specialist, and he tells me that something that once would cost thousands of pounds can often now be booked for a couple of hundred. And that is in well-known publications; advertising in local newspapers can now be very affordable.

Love junk - Leaflets and Unaddressed mail

I should also mention leaflets because they still have a place in your marketing armoury. It's not for everyone, but year after year, the stats are compelling. According to Royal Mail,

- 92% of people read the door drops delivered to their home by Royal Mail

- 59% of people have visited a company's website to find out more after receiving a door drop

- 67% of people were prompted to make a purchase as a result of receiving a door drop

- 79% of recipients either keep, read quickly or pass on to someone else leaflets that they receive

Not only that, they have simple but proven benefits:

- Leaflets are a highly affordable and cost-effective way to market your brand, especially when compared to other forms of print and digital advertising

- With good copywriting you can convey key messages and information easily

- With creativity you can get people's attention quickly and engage them

- You can target very specific demographics

- People often pin your leaflet to a board in a highly visible part of their home

If you are sceptical about this because in your house every leaflet that comes through the letter box goes straight into the recycling – that is because they were not targeted well enough, creative or didn't engage with what truly matters to you. Remember what we said about websites earlier? They must be precisely targeted to be effective.

With care and effort, leafleting can be very powerful.

Out and about - Trade Shows, County Shows, Fetes and Wedding Fayres

Another permutation on the events theme is to attend and exhibit at trade shows and wedding fayres.

Taking the latter first, I have written a book on how to make an amazing wedding speech, and an obvious place to promote it is at wedding fayres. I think I have done this on six occasions and each time there were mortgage advice firms present.

Be visible where your target market is, as they say.

Trade and County shows are another great opportunity – trade shows because if you target a specific market or niche, then prospects will be present in their hundreds if not thousands. County shows because if your business is predominantly local, then again tens of thousands of people have the opportunity to see your stand/stall or booth.

One of my brothers is a professional family portrait photographer, and whilst he doesn't have a stand at his county show, he does set one up at his local village fete. He tells me that *"...the pitch is £35 and business is always very good. Oh, and I get an advertisement on the village fete website too."*

Again, I have often bumped into financial adviser businesses at county shows and village fetes – often sharing pitches with local estate agents, solicitors or accountants.

All in all, another inexpensive but effective way to get high visibility amongst your target market. But for *maximum* effectiveness, you should combine this low-tech tactic with high-tech and make sure that you complement your live presence with real-time social media posts that share images, videos and even live streaming of you and your team at the relevant show.

Add to Home Screen

Here's a fun one…

The internet is littered with stats on mobile phone use. It doesn't need an academic study to know that wherever we go – pubs, trains, public spaces, restaurants, football matches etc., people are staring at their devices. We just don't want to miss out on what's going on in the world.

One set of figures I saw recently, suggested that on average, adults look at their mobile phone 264 times per day. Other surveys say something similar, so I guess it is near enough, and there's a fair chance that some (or all) of your clients are within that group too.

So have you ever considered what an amazing opportunity their mobile phone home screen is as an advertising space for your financial advice business?

You are probably aware that you can add a link to any website directly to the home screen of your mobile phone, so why not suggest to your clients that they do just that. One financial planning firm has even created a short video which shows clients how to do that:

http://bit.ly/SerenityAddToHomeScreen

Again, as part of your onboarding process, walk clients through how they can add a link to your website to their mobile device, and with a bit of luck they will see it 264 times per day.

Feel the love - Review sites

It was inevitable that the financial advice equivalent of TripAdvisor was going to happen at some point. And when it did, I recall many IFAs initially turning their noses up at the idea.

When TripAdvisor first appeared in 2000, it was a game changer for the hospitality industry, and today very few of us haven't been positively or negatively influenced by a review on the site. For the first time, consumers were able to get the truth behind glossy websites for hotels, restaurants and destinations, and to learn what a venue is really like from other travellers.

Amazon too, provides consumers with reviews of products sold through the site, and the company works hard to ensure that reviews are genuine. Clearly on any review site there is potential for the system to be abused, but most people reading a range of feedback can form their own judgement on a product or service even if one or two reviews are potentially 'dodgy'.

So when VouchedFor first appeared on the scene in the UK, several financial advisers said to me:

"It's crazy for the sheer breadth of services we provide and expertise we have to be boiled down to a simple star rating."

Some might see an Amazon, TripAdvisor or Trustpilot type approach to be unfair or inappropriate to the business of financial advice, but that's the way the world is now and we have little choice but to embrace it. If we want consumers to find us online, then we need to be aware of and open to developments like this which can both manage our reputation but also generate new leads.

And if you are fortunate enough to have been highly rated through VouchedFor, you have a fantastic marketing opportunity. Coincidentally, only today I saw one financial planner posting on Facebook how proud he is to be included in VouchedFor's 2020 guide to the UK's top rated advisers. He said,

"Very chuffed to have been rated as one of the UK's highest rated financial advisers, and for my company being in the top 15!"

And the fact that VouchedFor's guide is included in the Times newspaper, adds an additional layer of credibility.

I saw this and thought of you...

From high-tech to the lowest possible tech you can get – the humble Post-it Note.

Whilst the possibilities with technology and social media are exciting, you still can't beat a very human touch and the Post-it Note fulfils this role very nicely.

When I was an Inspector/Broker Consultant in the mid-1980s, I met Alan, a high-flying financial adviser in Croydon who put aside a couple of minutes a day to look for articles and features in magazines and newspapers which he would tear out and send to relevant clients and prospects in the post.

The articles were on every topic imaginable from sport to travel and from music to wine making – whatever was appropriate to his clients' interests.

All he would do is write on a Post-it Note something like,

"Mike and Sue – I saw this and thought of you.

Best wishes Alan"

That's it. Tearing articles out of publications and sending them with a handwritten note was a core element of how he kept relationships moving with people.

He was one of the most successful financial advisers I have ever met. He told me once,

"It's so simple Phil – the most important part of the fact-find are the soft fact questions. People love that you thought of them and took the trouble to send something of interest. It's how I stand out from other financial advisers and gets me referrals all the time."

I rest my case.

A modern alternative?

The nearest I can think of is tagging a client when you see something of interest on social media. It has the same effect, but severely lacks the human touch.

A few years later Coutts & Co were part of my patch when I was at Zurich Life. They had a very high-end financial planning arm and were quite advanced at using technology within their business. But it was the occasional human touch that clients loved – something that Coutts were known for.

Whilst other banks were sending statements to their customers direct from a central processing office, Coutts would first send the statements to the relevant branch manager, who would often append a few handwritten remarks before it was sent out.

"Love to the family"

"Congratulations on your daughter's engagement"

"Enjoy your forthcoming cruise"

And perhaps occasionally,

"Please see me."

Red carpet treatment

Several years ago before social media, my wife and I decided to move house, so we did the tour of the local estate agents to see who would be best to sell our property.

We visited all five agents in the area and were promised their best service and a speedy sale. They were all pleasant enough with friendly staff and great testimonials. But what really struck me was that they were all identical.

They all looked the same, all offered an identical service and they all had much the same fees. They all said,

"We have decades of experience and will provide you with a fool-proof selling strategy that's tailored to you and proven to sell your home."

How were we to choose which one to go with?

Their testimonials were good, but there was no Facebook back then to get a second opinion. So we parked this at the back of our minds and forgot about it until the next day.

The very following day a brown envelope arrived in the post from one of the estate agents. On opening it, inside was nothing but an eight inch by six-inch piece of red carpet. There was no letter or anything else included – but stuck to the back of the piece of carpet was a simple message,

ALL OUR CLIENTS GET THE SAME TREATMENT

Call us today and we'll roll out the red carpet for you.

They got the job.

That's about as old-school a marketing idea that you can think of. Simple, effective and differentiated them from the other agents.

I'll give you that idea for free.

But a year ago this simple idea resurfaced, when I saw the approach being used by another business, but this time the estate agent had added a modern twist with an additional message,

ALL OUR CLIENTS GET THE SAME TREATMENT

Call us today and we'll roll out the red carpet for you.

Take a selfie holding your red carpet – then post it on social media tagging us. When you do, we'll give you an extra 5% discount.

Again, a brilliant example of bring an old idea right up to date to combine low tech with high tech.

Take it Personally

Personalised Marketing

All the talk in marketing circles right now is around personalisation, and clearly handwritten notes on bank statements, tagging people on social media and sending out newspaper clippings with Post-it Notes all tick that box.

According to Salesforce (state of the Connected Consumer):

- 55% of consumers and 75% of companies expect businesses to send them personalised offers

- 58% of consumers and 70% of companies say it is critical or very important for businesses to provide a personalised experience

- 52% of consumers and 65% of companies will consider switching brands if businesses do not personalise communications with them

And according to McKinsey, personalisation can deliver five to eight times the ROI on total marketing spends with 88% of US marketers seeing measurable improvements as a result.

Personalisation and hyper-personalisation tends to be a marketing strategy used by (often) larger companies whereby through data analysis and digital technology they can offer individual offers and messages to consumers and prospects. But it need not be the domain of just larger businesses.

For smaller financial advice businesses it can be as simple as including a client's first name at the start and within the body of your email newsletter. But make sure you test it before you send it out – how many times have you received an email that began,

"Dear %%FIRST_NAME%%"

Personalisation isn't always about putting someone's name on something. It is also about making sure that communications are both **timely and relevant**.

Remember Alan's Post-it Note example earlier? What he sent out was timely and relevant – you can do this too through email newsletters and updates that are appropriate to individual clients.

And don't forget postcards too! Whole books have been written about the power of sending postcards that are highly personalised. Use them as part of your overall communications package with clients to:

- Send personalised reminders about forthcoming meetings or events
- Follow up after meetings
- Send as an invitation or ticket for an event
- Send quick personalised thank you messages
- Send quick messages of congratulations
- Send messages that are quick and to the point
- Send as a gift certificate
- Get quick feedback on something you are doing or have done

Another easy thing that financial advisers can do is to make sure that your website presence is relevant to different types of visitors. This doesn't (yet) mean having a website that is akin to Amazon where everyone sees a different home page, but it can be as simple as having different sites for prospects and existing clients. And we could include professional introducers too in that differentiation.

The relationship that a prospect has with an adviser is very different from that of an existing client. As an existing client, my relationship with you is not just face to face, and as part of your proposition to me I would like to see content online that is exclusive to me and other clients.

Ideally, a financial advice firm should have separate website strategies for each of the following:

- Prospecting
- Client retention
- Client upsells

Alan was also right when he said that the soft fact section of your fact find is incredibly important. Collecting data about hobbies, interests, travel and much more, all help an adviser to customise and tailor their communications. For those of you with clients on social media, you can often pick up valuable clues as to what they are interested in.

If they are on Twitter, take a look at the accounts they follow and note their interests. If they are on

Facebook, very often you can see their interests and much more when you look at their About tab. And if they are on LinkedIn, you can often see information on their business interests.

All of this is freely available invaluable information which with a great deal of care, you can use to personalise their experience with you and your business.

Take the time to also learn about your clients' communication preferences. Again at the fact find end of the relationship you should consider asking them if they like to use messaging tools such as WhatsApp, Facebook Messenger, Google Hangouts, Facetime, Skype, Zoom etc. What about their traditional communication preferences like letters, email, telephone and SMS?

All too often we communicate with clients in the way that is most comfortable and easy for *us*, but wherever possible and practicable we should aim to communicate in a way that is most comfortable for the client.

If you haven't collected this information at the fact find stage, you still have different opportunities to do so. Increasingly financial advisers run client surveys or even client focus groups where you can ask for this information. Client surveys are really important for advice firms, though the only downside is that they can be a little tedious, particularly if it is going to take twenty-five minutes to wade through. However, if you flag up to clients as part of your onboarding process that you send out an annual client survey, they will come to expect it at some point. Make sure too that you incentivise people to complete it by offering a gift.

You can also have a permanent client survey running on your client-facing website, so they can complete it at any time, but with gentle prompts from you once a year. Tools such as SurveyMonkey will do the job nicely.

Personalisation in marketing and communications will become more and more important if we are to differentiate ourselves and our businesses. New ideas and software are being produced all the time, so watch this one become a big thing in adviser marketing over the coming years.

Keeping the Plates Spinning

Email Newsletter

We have mentioned newsletters and email newsletters several times in passing, but it's worth nailing this one down a little more.

Whilst all of us probably admit to receiving too much email every day, that's for the most part our own fault. Discounting spam email, we almost certainly signed up to receive it at some point ourselves, and we do that because it is an easy way to be kept updated about things that we are interested in. And regardless of the popularity of social media, email still has a remarkable ability to cut through it all, and it isn't going away any time soon.

Many commentators predicted in August 2003 that traditional telephony was about to die, with the arrival of Skype. Why would anyone want to pay for phone calls when we could talk for free using the latest technology? And the same people are predicting the end of email

It is true that messaging through apps such as Facebook Messenger and What's App has grown massively in popularity, but in reality all that has done is to give us choices in how we communicate with people, with most of us using a variety of apps depending on the situation at the time and the person we want to talk to.

But telephone and email are still with us, with many professional marketers saying that email is still all powerful when it comes to business communications and marketing.

That does of course depend on your type of business and what it is that you sell. We also have GDPR to be conscious of, so it would be wrong to say that email is necessarily the panacea of marketing for IFAs – but it is still very useful.

For financial advisers, the key benefits in terms of email marketing are:

- A quick and easy way to deliver eGuides and welcome messages to people who engage with our website

- An easy way to start building a relationship with these people days and weeks after they have engaged with your website, through a sequence of messages

- Strengthening relationships and adding value to existing clients

- Email newsletters can generate phone calls or other immediate activity (sign-ups for your seminar, visits to specific pages on your website, donations to your charity etc.)

- Proof that your business is active, busy and has something to say

- Get feedback on initiatives you have underway or questions that you have for your client community

- Build and strengthen your brand

- Learn what content you communicate encourages the most engagement, through your email newsletter metrics

- It's easy to set up and all but free to send

- You can reach clients on any of their devices

- You can send different email newsletters to clients with different interests (see relevance earlier)

- Build excitement about something you have coming up

- Promote other services or products that you have on your value ladder

- Attract referrals and website visits when people pass on your newsletter to others

- Keep your business front of mind

- Opt-outs clean your list and improve the overall quality of your recipient pool

- They can be pre-scheduled in advance

- And more...

Most financial advisers will not be purchasing lists of email addresses, so we can ignore email for cold prospecting, and there would also be GDPR implications.

So advisers will for the most part be using email as a marketing tool to engage with website visitors and to add value to existing clients.

When we first started LifeTalk, we attracted three or four hundred financial advisers to our online group pretty quickly, and we would send them an email newsletter once a month as a kind of summary/update. As soon as we sent out the email, recipients would almost instantly log in to the site.

A few months later, a technology expert asked me why I didn't send out the email newsletter more often, and I said instantly that my IFA audience wouldn't want that. He suggested that I give it a try – to the extent that we initially go to once a week and subsequently every day.

I had serious doubts about this but did it anyway.

The move to a weekly newsletter had an immediate effect, with more people logging in more often. We also had no opt outs at all. When we moved to daily, I was poised ready for multiple opt outs. Out of an email list of a thousand advisers at the time, only two people opted out.

But what also happened was that as soon as we sent out the email newsletter, huge numbers of advisers responded by logging into the site almost immediately, and it had a massive impact on site visitor numbers.

In short, the more email we sent out, the more people engaged with us and our site.

It goes without saying that what you send out has to be high value and high quality, and you also have to learn through trial and error how long the email needs to be and the type of content that you include.

In today's world, once a month is not enough to keep the relationship plates spinning and once a day is probably too much. Once a week looks to be spot on – but guess what – why don't you ask your clients when they come on board what *they* would like. Give them a sample of the content you send out and put them on the appropriate list for the frequency they prefer. That's easy with today's email tools.

And as I've said before, stay on top of your numbers. Almost all email newsletter services will give you the essentials, such as:

- How many emails arrived
- How many and which ones bounced
- How many were opened and by whom
- Who didn't open their email
- Which links in the email newsletter were clicked
- How many and who unsubscribed
- How many were forwarded to someone else
- Spam reports

Just like your website stats, you must stay on top of these numbers because they give you amazing insights; what's more they guide you towards content and frequencies that are right for *your* clients.

Once you have decided to send out a regular email newsletter, you need to commit to it because it is the predictability and consistency that counts – a bit like blogging.

With that said, I would be inclined to take some time to research your choice of email newsletter provider (there are many to choose from and some marketing agencies for advisers can also do it for you). I would also be inclined to create specimen content of different lengths, styles and topics, and enlist the help of a small test group of clients to get their feedback before going live.

Finally – and the icing on the cake; why not try something a little different and send a **video email newsletter**, where you embed a video of you speaking the content right into your email.

Once again, BombBomb is your solution at https://bombbomb.com.

Keep it Professional

Professional Connections

There are various schools of thoughts on the effectiveness of building relationships with local accountants, solicitors, bank managers and estate agents. Most financial advisers have attracted some business through this route, but in recent years it has become less and less reliable as a source of leads for a variety of reasons, and to this end advisers are missing a huge opportunity.

Back in the 1980s and 1990s most financial advisers had strong relationships with local professionals, which were often founded on a mutual interest in golf, tennis or organisations like Rotary and Chamber of Commerce. Beer also figured highly…

Like many things when it comes to marketing, strategy is important. Simply meeting an accountant at a local event and agreeing to be mindful of each other's services isn't going to cut it. Building relationships with local professionals needs thinking about **and a plan**.

You may remember from earlier when I was speaking at the Asia Pacific Financial Planning conference in Singapore. Financial advisers from Australia, New Zealand, Singapore, Malaysia and India were all in attendance and there to network and share best practice. I got talking to Robbie, an adviser who told me that his firm was the largest financial advice business in Australia and New Zealand and that he put it all down to building strategic relationships with accountants – with the emphasis on the word strategic.

In passing, Robbie told me,

"Building relationships with professional introducers is critical, but financial advisers in the UK pay lip service to this."

I asked if he could expand on what he meant, and he explained to me that in order to attract high quality leads from accountants, he needed to offer them something of high value, and that turned out to be training. To be specific, training on how to be a financial planner. I thought about this and asked why he would want to train accountants to be financial planners – was this a master plan to grow his business by taking over an accountancy firm with a financial planning arm that worked to his own model?

"No" he said.

"And there is no risk of them becoming competitors either. What they value is the training – the new skill set. Accountants have had their chance to be financial planners and chosen not to take it. But they do value professional development in all its forms, and I'm happy to invest in it because when they know in detail what a financial planner really does, the quality of the relationship and the leads that they will pass to us will be second to none."

Which all makes a lot of sense.

Colin Low is a Chartered Financial Planner and founder of Kingsfleet Wealth in Ipswich and an expert on building relationships with professional connections.

Watch this video of me interviewing him about his five-step approach to building relationships from our Financial Adviser Mastermind & Challenge video series:

http://bit.ly/ColinLow

A Powerhouse of Opportunity

LinkedIn

I'm going to look at LinkedIn in some detail because it is a powerhouse of opportunity for financial advisers. What follows is literally what really works on LinkedIn and how to use it without wasting time.

Before going any further, it is really important that you have a clear idea on *why* you are using LinkedIn in the first place.

The vast majority of financial advisers on LinkedIn waste a great deal of time 'floundering' around on the platform without having a clear idea of what they are trying to achieve.

Each time they log in to the site or app, they move around without any clear direction or purpose, so the point of this chapter is to give you a clear strategy and approach.

For most financial advisers on LinkedIn, whether employed or self-employed, the best outcome will usually result from people visiting your profile.

You therefore need to:

1. Create and position your LinkedIn profile so that it **speaks directly to your ideal client** or connection

2. Draw attention from the LinkedIn algorithm so that **it supports, rewards and promotes you and your**

expertise

3. Draw attention from your ideal client or connection **so that they want to visit your profile**

4. Engage with people who visit your profile **in a way that starts conversations**

The tips that follow are designed to help you easily achieve all of the above. But first, let's get some clarity on *why* you are on LinkedIn by answering the following questions:

Describe yourself and your financial advice business

_____
_____
_____
_____
_____
_____
_____
_____
_____
_____
_____
_____
_____

Describe your **ideal** client or connection

_____
_____
_____
_____
_____
_____
_____
_____
_____
_____
_____
_____

Why are you targeting these people and what problems do they have that you can solve?

_____
_____
_____
_____
_____
_____
_____
_____
_____
_____
_____
_____

How many of them are on LinkedIn? (Hint: use the search tool)

_____

_____

_____

_____

_____

_____

_____

_____

_____

_____

_____

_____

What do they post status updates about?

_____

_____

_____

_____

_____

_____

_____

_____

_____

_____

_____

What articles do they post on LinkedIn and what themes/topics do they cover?

_____

_____

_____

_____

_____

_____

_____

_____

_____

_____

_____

_____

What hashtags are they using with their posts and comments?

_____

_____

_____

_____

_____

_____

_____

_____

_____

_____

_____

_____

What LinkedIn groups have they joined?

_____
_____
_____
_____
_____
_____
_____
_____
_____
_____
_____
_____

Do they have LinkedIn Company Pages, and if so, what content do they post there?

_____
_____
_____
_____
_____
_____
_____
_____
_____
_____
_____

Do they have a Showcase Page on LinkedIn and if so, what do they post about there?

_____
_____
_____
_____
_____
_____
_____
_____
_____
_____
_____
_____

Are they promoting any events on LinkedIn and if so what type of events are they promoting?

_____
_____
_____
_____
_____
_____
_____
_____
_____
_____
_____
_____

What is your primary area of expertise?

_____
_____
_____
_____
_____
_____
_____
_____
_____
_____
_____
_____

What is your ideal result from using LinkedIn and how does that help you to achieve your goals for the year/next five years etc?

_____
_____
_____
_____
_____
_____
_____
_____
_____
_____
_____
_____

What did you notice about these questions?

Yes, they are more about understanding how your target market uses LinkedIn than about yourself.

When you really get to know your ideal connections on LinkedIn, you are giving yourself a significantly improved chance of attracting more of the leads and clients that you really want.

It also helps to focus the mind on posting content that is relevant to their needs.

Answering these questions often forces people to think much more clearly about how they use LinkedIn to attract their ideal connections, and you will find that almost straight away you will have more focus in your use of the site.

So far so good...

Recommended actions

Next, there are certain hygiene factors that we need to put in place – not least of which is that your personal LinkedIn profile needs to be fit for purpose.

1. Financial Advisers should have a **fully completed personal profile** that is keyword optimised throughout and it should have been written to address the primary problems, needs or characteristics of your main target market.

2. You should also have searched for and followed up to ten hashtags that are used by or are highly relevant to your target market. Go to LinkedIn home and search (for example) #Retirement and then click the Follow button. Follow other hashtags that you know are of interest to your target market. E.g. #Golf.

3. You should also have joined any special interest groups on LinkedIn where your target market hangs out. Don't forget that these will also include groups related to their work, business or personal interests – not necessarily personal finance related.

   For example, there are over 3,000 groups on LinkedIn for people interested in golf; almost 3,000 related to football and around 80 related to fishing. There are over 28,000 groups related to leadership and most of these groups have memberships in the thousands.

4. You should also have created and optimised your Company Page on LinkedIn.

   Useful but not essential:

1. Signed up for Premium membership
2. Created a Showcase page on LinkedIn

Note: Nothing I am about to describe requires the use of LinkedIn Premium membership.

Premium membership's key benefit in the context of lead generation is that with the free version you are able to see the last five people who looked at your profile, and with Premium, you can see everyone who has looked at you over the last ninety days.

So if you log in every day, you will over time be fully up to speed on who is looking at your profile. Keep reading to understand why this is so important.

Getting Started

The Golden Five areas of activity each day.

Your ideal daily LinkedIn activity is divided into five parts:

1. Check profile visits and engage with people – send and reply to messages

2. Post status updates

3. Comment on other people's content

4. Comment on content around followed hashtags

5. Post Company Status Updates

Let's look at each in turn.

Part 1: Profile Visits and Engaging with People

People who visit your profile have done so deliberately. (Note: It is possible that it will have been an automated visit using external software tools, but the vast majority of visits to your profile will have been done manually by the person themselves as a result of finding you on LinkedIn.)

These visits to your profile represent a valuable opportunity to **start conversations** that begin through the LinkedIn messaging system, but which progress to email, telephone, Skype/Zoom or a meeting in a coffee shop.

In my view, the feature which shows who has visited your profile is one of, if not *the* most powerful tool on LinkedIn to start the process of generating new leads and enquiries.

To maximise the likelihood of conversations taking place, you should follow this approach:

First, check who viewed your LinkedIn profile and then look at their profile.

As you look at their profile consider:

- What do you both have in common?
- Why do you think they looked at you?
- Say 'thank you' to them by sending a personalised connection request if not already connected*
- Say 'thank you' to them if you are already connected: *"What prompted you to stop by?"*

*I have had financial advisers tell me that they attracted high value new investment and pension clients the

very first time they said 'thank you' to strangers who visited their profile.

Consider using these scripts (they work very well for me):

Script 1

Hi Sue…

Many thanks for taking a look at my profile – I see that we have some mutual connections. Please let me know if I can introduce you to anyone else in my network.

In the meantime, it would be great to connect.

Thanks in advance…

Regards

Phil

Script 2

Hi Sue…

Many thanks for taking a look at my profile again – I hope you found something of interest and that things are going well for you.

May I ask what prompted you to drop by?

Thanks in advance…

Regards

Phil

In many cases, people will actually reply to you, so you should then take the opportunity to engage with them in conversation – building on any areas of common interest.

If they accept your connection request but don't reply, send another message thanking them for connecting, and politely asking what prompted them to connect.

Want to stand out from the crowd?

Once you are connected to someone, if enabled on your LinkedIn app, you will be able to not only send written messages, but also audio and video messages to people.

This is a powerful and proven way for financial advisers to differentiate themselves, because very few people use these messaging features on LinkedIn.

Again, avoid being self-promotional in these messages. Your aim is to **engage with people with a view to starting a conversation**. Leave the salesy stuff to further down the line when the relationship is maturing.

Part 2: Status Updates

Each day, post a short observational or story-based status update around something you did, noticed, thought about, watched, heard etc. over the last twenty-four hours. Try to avoid including a hyperlink to somewhere that is off LinkedIn e.g. your blog or website.

Status Updates are designed to draw people's attention to you so that they go on to look at your profile.

Follow these tips to maximise potential from the LinkedIn algorithm:

- Avoid making your post promotional

- Try to write your content so that it encourages interaction and conversations between readers, so occasionally ask a question at the end of your post. 'Engagement probability' is an important driver of the LinkedIn algorithm

- Occasionally post about news within the financial planning industry – or news within your target market's industry

- Occasionally use infographics to highlight points you are making

- Occasionally go deep and niche on topics in your posts

- Remember that 'people buy people', so aim for human content occasionally – include emotion, humour, nostalgia etc.

- Highlight your expertise without selling – include short tips, inside information and case studies. Educational content is great too.

- Post content that you know your target audience cares about. How relevant your content is to them is a key driver of the LinkedIn algorithm.

- Occasionally tag companies and individuals in your posts – more as a way to highlight their skills, expertise and services rather than to get their attention.

   As a financial adviser, occasionally you might want to mention or tag local professional connections.

- Publicly thank people for their help – use the LinkedIn Kudos tool

- Use native and live video as posts

- Post about events that you have attended or that you are at right now

- Include three relevant hashtags on your post

- Monitor which times of day get the most engagement on your posts

Notes:

Aim for a minimum of one status update *every* weekday, but three spread over a day is even better.

Consider posting at weekends too, though not essential.

Share your post to Twitter. This can be automated if you have included your Twitter information in your contact details.

Time required per post: one to three minutes – possibly longer if you need to create a fancy infographic.

Plan your posts in advance if you have time.

Take note of what LinkedIn themselves say:

"Genuine conversation around real experiences spark better and deeper conversation. Better conversation, in turn, leads to stronger community and connection."

Part 3: Comment on other people's posts on the main home news feed

By commenting on other people's posts, you are sending a signal to the LinkedIn algorithm that you are a networker and not a broadcaster, and as a result you will be rewarded with greater visibility, and more often than not, more profile visits.

Here's what you should do:

- Scroll through your news feed and pick out interesting content from other people – particularly people in your prime target market or their industry/profession

- Avoid salesy comments – keep it simple, such as "Great post Sue – thanks for the heads up" or "Thanks for the useful insights John – extremely valuable"

- Do not post anything self-promotional

- Add up to three relevant hashtags to your comments. So in the example above, your comment might look something like this:

  "Thanks for the useful insights John – extremely valuable. #retirement #lifestyle

- If you really don't have any comments to make, then 'Like' other people's posts – even this will help draw attention to you

Notes:

Add comments to three posts each day. More if you wish. Time required per comment: 30 seconds max.

Part 4: Comment on other people's posts that revolve around a saved/followed hashtag

LinkedIn is conscious that far too many people simply broadcast content on the platform, so the LinkedIn algorithm is now rewarding people who **interact and engage with others around areas of common interest**.

Follow the actions below, and you will send a message to the LinkedIn algorithm that you are a networker and not a broadcaster.

Yes, broadcasting has its place, but if you want more people to visit your profile so that you can start conversations, you should play the LinkedIn game and follow their rules.

When you do, you will be rewarded with greater visibility and more profile visits. Your comments will also be more visible to other people who follow specific hashtags.

Here's what you should do:

- Visit your list of saved/followed hashtags. On mobile, tap on your photo on the home feed; this opens a side bar where you will find your followed hashtags. On desktop, your followed hashtags are on the left side of your home screen (both these may be subject to change by LinkedIn).

- Tap/click on a hashtag used by your target audience.

- Scroll down the news feed for that hashtag and add short comments such as "Great post Sue – thanks for the heads up" or "Thanks for the useful insights John – extremely valuable".

- Do not post anything self-promotional in your comments.

- Add up to three relevant hashtags to your comment – ideally one of which is the hashtag that you are currently viewing. So if you are commenting on a post in the feed for (say) #Leadership, you could post something like:

"Thanks for sharing Susan – you've made some great points there. #Leadership #Management

#Change"

- If you really don't have any comments to make, then 'Like' other people's posts – even this will help draw attention to you. But commenting is always the best course of action.

Notes:

Add comments to three posts each day. More if you wish. Time required per comment: 30 seconds max.

Part 5: Company Status Updates

Post a short observational or story-based status update around something you did, noticed, thought about, watched, heard etc. over the last twenty-four hours. Try to avoid including a hyperlink to somewhere that is off LinkedIn e.g. your blog or website.

Tips:

- Try to follow a theme in your posts that is related to your company's expertise – perhaps have a weekly or monthly theme.

- Avoid making your post promotional, though one post per week that is promotional is fine.

- Try to write your content so that it encourages interaction and engagement by readers, so occasionally ask a question at the end of your post.

- Occasionally post about news in your industry.

- Occasionally use infographics to highlight points you are making.

- Remember that 'people buy people' (even on Company Pages), so aim for human content occasionally – include emotion, humour, nostalgia etc.

- Show your expertise without selling – include short tips, inside information, educational content and client case studies.

- Occasionally tag companies and individuals in your posts – more as a way to highlight their skills, expertise and services rather than to get their attention.

- Publicly thank people for their help – perhaps a local professional connection.

- Use native and live video as posts.

- Post about events that you have attended or that you are at right now. Make these a mixture of local events, your own events and financial services industry events (there's no shortage of them!)

- Include three relevant hashtags on your post.

Notes:

Aim for a minimum of one Company Page status update per day, every weekday - but three spread over a day is even better.

Consider posting at weekends too, though not essential.

Time required per post: one to three minutes – possibly longer if you need to create a fancy infographic. Longer if you are streaming a live video.

Live video on Company Pages is highly recommended and can dramatically increase views.

If you have colleagues, make a point of telling them that something has been posted on your Company Page, and encourage them to Like, Comment and Share your posts so that your reach on LinkedIn is significantly extended.

Plan your posts in advance if you have time.

Optional additional daily activity

- Post articles
- Comment on other people's articles
- Post Showcase page updates
- Post content in LinkedIn groups
- Comment on other people's content in LinkedIn Groups
- Search for ideal clients, reach out and connect

Notes:

For maximum traction, your own articles need to be long, detailed, deep on expertise, niche, factual and include unique insights. Therefore these are time-consuming but potentially high value.

Showcase Page updates should follow the same approach as Company Page updates.

Avoid self-promotional content in Groups – aim to add value at all times.

Consider starting your own Group on LinkedIn. This is a very powerful way to generate leads, though is time consuming and should be seen as a long-term strategy.

Many LinkedIn users think that searching for ideal clients, reaching out and connecting should be high on the priority list of daily activities. It can be but is not generally as effective as the five key activities described in this chapter. The tactics we have highlighted throughout are intended to draw these people *to you*, rather than you going to them - making it much easier to strike up conversations with them.

Kittens in Boxes

Facebook

In 2003 Mark Zuckerberg and his co-founders initially limited the site's membership to Harvard students and later students at Columbia, Stanford, and Yale.

The rest, as they say is history and at September 2019, the site had 2.45 billion active monthly users. At the time of writing Facebook is the fourth most popular site on the internet, but the one which people spend most time on – typically 17.3 minutes per day.

It didn't take the business world very long to cotton on to the fact that you could essentially get free advertising – and with all those people on there, it was bound to be an easy way to market your business.

It was in the early days.

And still is today if you know how to play. Multiple businesses worldwide make millions a year simply through Facebook advertising. It is possible to make money purely through organic use of the site, but today you really need to pay to see anything like the returns you would hope for.

However, relatively few financial advisers are convinced by Facebook as a marketing tool. I recently ran a straw poll amongst seventy IFAs/advisers on Facebook and asked:

Is Facebook (paid or otherwise) a good source of leads & inquiries for your financial advice business?

- 47.5% said that they didn't know and hadn't tried it

- 32.5% said no and that it was a waste of time for their business

- 15% said that they had got the occasional lead and could probably do better with some effort

- 4% said they could rely on Facebook to produce all the leads they needed through both paid and organic promotions

So 80% of those polled said that Facebook was not a good source of leads, paid or otherwise.

One IFA added that he found it very good for recruiting, whilst another said that it is not for business use and more for socialising.

Another said she likes Facebook for all the kitten videos…

By contrast, when I ran a similar straw poll with predominantly mortgage and protection advisers, slightly over 55% told me that they found Facebook invaluable as a lead generation tool but adding that they could probably do even better with more effort.

So mixed views, but not entirely unpredictable.

When advisers attend my marketing workshops, a common question that does come up is if they were to run

Facebook ads, how much should they be spending on advertising.

It's a good question with a very simple answer. In essence, it is first about figuring out what sort of ad will turn one pound in advertising costs into two pounds of sales, or five or ten or a hundred – as long as it is more than the amount you put in.

Once you are earning more out of your advertising than you are putting in, your advertising budget can be as high (or as low) as you wish. If you pay £10 in advertising costs and earn (say) £100 in sales, you can safely increase your budget.

But what many people find is that they spend £10 on advertising and only get £5 back in sales. In which case your offer and advertisement still need more work. The offer and its copywriting is all important here.

When you know what offer you have to make through the right advertisement and can get two pounds or more back for every one pound you put in, then the world is your oyster. So it is all about the quality and effectiveness of the ad. Work on this first, split test with a small budget until you are making a positive gain.

Facebook makes it easy to get traction for your advertisements too, by the fact that a massive proportion of your target market is likely to be using the site from time to time – and that you can target specific types of people at a granular level.

And as we all know, when people look at a product on Amazon or somewhere else, the next time they visit Facebook there's an advertisement for that very same product. It's called retargeting, and financial advisers can do it too by using the Facebook Pixel.

It's a little piece of code that you add to your website and which follows your visitors' movements, enabling you to show an advertisement to them when they next visit Facebook. This is clever stuff, because as we've gone to great lengths to say in this book, consistency and continuity is important. Good advertising needs a certain amount of repetition until it hits home.

The Facebook Pixel also gives you data on the performance of your ads, so that you can modify them accordingly. The more you test your advertisements the greater the likelihood that you can keep tweaking them until they work.

Another powerful option is that Facebook can create 'lookalike audiences' for you to target based on the characteristics (interests, demographics, likes etc.) of people who have already interacted with your website or advertisements.

The Pixel can do a lot more too, but this is a good place to start if you haven't yet considered using Facebook advertising.

You can learn how to do it yourself, there are a multitude of resources on Facebook itself, plus videos on YouTube. But ideally you need to find a Facebook advertising expert who knows the system inside out. Really you should find someone who already generates leads for other professional services businesses. If not, try Fiverr, Upwork and other outsourcing sites.

There are also a small but increasing number of marketing agencies who specifically work with financial advisers, but you always need to ask what experience and success they have had with Facebook advertising.

Should I boost my posts?

When posting on your business page on Facebook, you will probably have seen the 'Boost Post' button. By spending a tenner or more you are offered the chance for hundreds, if not thousands more people to see your post, but most professional marketers suggest that you are to some extent wasting your money when you use the Boost button.

Ideally you should start an advertisement from scratch because the copy in ads is usually very different from the copy in day to day posts, and also by simply boosting posts you are not leveraging the full power of Facebook's advertising platform. Always use Facebook's Ads Manager to create your advertisements.

Facebook groups

If you still don't want to pay to advertise on Facebook, you can also use it to find groups of people who match your target market. There are groups on the site for every type of person, interest and demographic imaginable, many of which have thousands of members.

If you target people who play the trumpet, you will find groups for trumpeters which have 150 posts per day. If you target people who love Chelsea football club, there is one group on Facebook with over 300,000 members – you get the idea. Go where your target market hangs out.

Just as you would when joining a group on LinkedIn, don't go in with all guns blazing. Simply look around, assess the tone of the group and interact with other people's content and add value. Don't try to promote yourself; the idea is to join the community, become part of it and gradually create curiosity over time. It's a long-haul strategy but is very powerful and one that is used by many successful businesses.

You could also create your *own* group on Facebook, just as I did for one of my target markets – financial advisers. The group revolves around your topic of interest and will over time attract more people to it. Through regular posting of value, your members will gradually show more and more interest in what you have to offer as a business.

If this is of interest to you as a tactic, it will be worth re-reading the chapter on Online Communities.

Create curiosity

It's worth mentioning curiosity again, because it is at the heart of generating leads without paying for advertisements on social media – whether you are using Facebook, LinkedIn, Twitter, Instagram or whatever.

If you are not going to pay to play on these sites, then creating curiosity is your best strategy. Don't just promote your services for free simply because you can – that is the fastest way to lose followers. Instead, interact, engage and add value to people's online experience – and do it with the expectation of receiving nothing in return.

You've heard that before in this book, haven't you. It's called networking – and over time great networkers create curiosity in others, and it is only a matter of time until they start to want to know more about you.

In my view, this is the only real way to attract business on Facebook without paying for advertisements. Be nice, be helpful, be fun, be likeable, be courteous, be valuable – be referable.

Is my target market on Facebook?

The numbers suggest they are - take a look at this graphic provided by Facebook and clearly the overall market is colossal. But even when you take just a small section of it that is more typical of many financial adviser businesses such as 55 to 64-year-olds, it's clear to see they are not only on Facebook, but they are active users.

Age and Gender
Self-reported information from people in their Facebook Profiles. Information only available for people aged 18 and older.

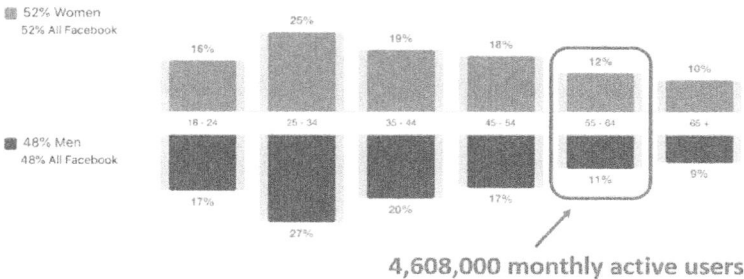

4,608,000 monthly active users

What about Twitter and Instagram?

Let's look at these two together because they have similarities for financial advisers.

Twitter and Instagram are micro-blogging platforms which double as search engines, and whilst some financial advisers have told me that they get the occasional enquiry through them, they are few and far between. Twitter seemed to work much better as a lead generation tool for advisers in its early days, but less so now.

Twitter can be a bit like the Wild West at the best of times and quite easy to get drawn into spats – I've seen several financial advisers doing this and it's not pretty. Better, to use it in much the same way that I described above – to add value and help people out, and so create curiosity.

Where Twitter and Instagram do work well is in support of and to complement other marketing activities that you are running. For instance, you can create Instagram ads directly within Facebook, so you get continuity across two platforms.

Whether you use just images or post Stories (a series of images or videos in a slideshow format) on Instagram, it's a great platform to support other initiatives that you have on the go elsewhere – again to get consistency and continuity. Perhaps you are hosting a seminar, so use it to post photos or videos of people at your event.

If you are sponsoring a local football team or even a roundabout, post some fun images. If you have written a blog on your website or elsewhere, use Instagram to post a quotation from it and add some relevant hashtags because people also use the platform as a search engine.

Maybe your latest Podcast has just come out – use Instagram to post an image of (say) your guest or interviewee.

If you use Instagram, you may have noticed that you cannot post clickable links within individual posts, with the link in your biography being the only place with a live URL. A neat tool to get around this is to use Linktree which gives you one link but with multiple destinations, one of which could be your blog.

So the link I use in my Instagram profile is https://linktr.ee/philipcalvert and this takes visitors to a choice of my destinations. Yes, you could also use this in your LinkedIn profile – or anywhere else for that matter.

One thing I have observed about Twitter is that it is a great platform to use as a search engine where you follow particular topics via hashtags to which you add your own comments, expertise and opinions. Again this creates curiosity.

Twitter has also proved to be a powerful platform for financial advisers to network with each other, and in many ways that is how it is used most by the profession. And on multiple occasions I have seen advisers recommending each other to journalists and others when their expertise is needed.

Finally, an aspect of Twitter that is particularly useful is the stats section on your profile. If you go into the analytics section of your profile, you will find some valuable information on the performance of your overall account and individual tweets. If you have a Twitter account, go to this link and dig around:

https://analytics.twitter.com/user/username/home

Look out for tweets that have performed well through impressions and engagement, and over time you will be able to see which type of content works best for you. Then post more content like that.

Hide and Seek

SEO or Search Engine Optimisation

As we near the end of this book, it's worth saying a few words on a topic which underpins much of what has already been written.

SEO can unfortunately be a bit of a dark art, with every marketer in the world having an opinion on what works and what doesn't. The truth is, only a few engineers at Google, Bing and other search engines *really* know what works to get you to the top of their list.

Paying is one way. Optimising your website and social media activity is another, and the latter is what we're going to look at.

It is said that there is enough publicly available information from Google for anyone to optimise their website effectively, but many internet marketers have added their own thoughts, ideas and opinions through extensive trial and error. Their skill is taking the information that is freely available and then creating strategies for fully leveraging it.

The problem is, from time to time Google engineers will tweak their search algorithm to put more emphasis on one aspect than another. So you might have put in a lot of effort, only to find you have plummeted in search results overnight.

There are however a few points that are almost always important to get right.

You will hopefully remember my mother-in-law Beryl from earlier who sat down with me in our kitchen to find an IFA in her area.

When we searched Google for "IFA in Guildford" I already knew which local advisers were on top of their SEO and who would be on page one of the results.

So here are some steps and tools that are particularly relevant to financial advisers:

Mobile

Firstly, your website must be optimised for viewing on a mobile device. A Google engineer said recently that if you were setting up a business from scratch today and putting your website together, you should start with all your focus on getting it to look good on an iPhone or other mobile device.

Here's a tool that you can use to check how your site currently looks on mobile:

https://search.google.com/test/mobile-friendly (This URL may change over time, but you should be able to find it on Google)

When you use it, you are also pinging Google and so alerting them to the existence of your site. If you haven't updated your site for a while, it is entirely possible that Google's search spiders have never visited it before, so doing this will not only tell you if your site is mobile friendly but will also remind them that you are out there.

Content

One way to attract Google's search spiders is to regularly add new content to your site. It is important to remember that Google is a service provider, and when people use their search engine to find information, Google likes to make sure that they find what they are looking for.

Financial advisers can increase their chances of appearing higher in search results by regularly posting content on their sites that includes keywords that people are searching for.

One technique to get better search positioning results and more site visitors, is to search for other financial advisers who are in your geographical area or who focus on your area of expertise or target market. Take a look at the sites that appear higher than yours and then do an audit of them.

Ask yourself what they are doing that you are not? You might also want to ask your website designer to look over their sites to see if there are any technical points you could learn from where they might have an edge over you.

Re-do the searches using different keywords and make a note of who appears where in the results. Again, if they are appearing higher than you, look closely to see what they are doing.

Then, if they have written any blog posts on a topic in which you have expertise, write your own blog or guide for your site - but do it better. Much better. Make it more thorough, more detailed, include better case studies and create custom graphics (see load speeds below). In other words, model what your competitors are doing but do it better. Remember to include your most important keywords throughout your blog or guide.

When you have written your in-depth blog or guide, promote it all over social media with links to it. Even better, send a message to high profile people within the profession or within other relevant industries and ask them if they would mention or share your article on their own social media. Yes, *ask people* for their help – it's amazing what happens!

If you approach other people, make sure that you nurture the relationships by helping them out in some way too by sharing *their* content.

There are software tools available that can monitor other sites in more depth, but simple searches will do for now.

Keywords

Content is important, but it's crucial to make sure that you are clear about the keywords that are associated with you as a business. For example, if you are a mortgage specialist and want to attract mortgage clients, you need to make sure that keywords and short phrases (aka long-tail keywords), are included in your website copy and within the code of your site. These are often known as tags and include the title of the site.

The content in the body of your site should also include headers or subtitles, which also include your keywords. That said, you need to be careful that you don't overuse certain keywords because Google will think you are spamming or 'keyword stuffing', and this may get your site penalised.

You will remember from earlier that more and more people are using voice devices to search the internet, and when doing so tend to speak more naturally than when typing. It can be tricky, but you need to strike a balance between getting your keywords in, but also acknowledging the natural language that people use when searching.

A useful tool to help you choose keywords for your area of expertise or target market is Keywords Everywhere at https://keywordseverywhere.com

This tells you how many people are searching for the keyword terms that are important to you, or for those that you want to be found. Useful, because there is little point in including keywords that no one is looking for…

With the growth of sites like Pinterest and Instagram, growth in image search is huge, so you also need to have your tags and keywords extend to the photos and images that you use on your site. In both the image file and within your website code you need to make sure that the images you use are labelled with your keywords and so able to be found in search results as well as the text on your site.

Backlinks

In its simplest form, it is important to have other websites linking to yours. Google takes the view that if another site has created a link to yours, then presumably your site is important or has value.

It is important that whilst you can have any site link to yours, it is better to have sites that are relevant and influential linking back to you. For example if you are an adviser and have had an article published in the online version of the FT (Financial Times) which includes a link to your website, Google will deem that to be a very high value backlink. Hence this is another reason why building relationships with journalists is important. See the earlier chapter on PR.

Even links from sites like LinkedIn can be valuable and also other people's blogs and podcasts where you are a contributor. If you are ever a guest on a podcast, ask the host if they can link to your website in their description or show notes.

Load speed

Slow performing websites are a pain for all concerned. Today's site visitors get impatient extremely quickly so even just from a usability perspective this is important to get right – but Google also looks at it too for search engine positioning.

The biggest contributor to slow load speeds is usually images with large file sizes, though you should also check that your website host is delivering high speeds. A professional website designer should know this, but it is always a good idea to check your site from time to time. This is another reason why it's a good idea to cull any images and content that is not needed on your site.

There are several freely available tools that you can use – simply search for 'site speed test' and you'll find some which will give recommendations for improvement. Google also has its own tool at https://developers.google.com/speed/pagespeed/insights

User experience

An extension of load speeds is the overall user experience. If people visit your site and bounce off because they can't find what they want or because the site is too cluttered, Google will penalise you in search result positioning.

Google looks at metrics such as:

- Bounce rate
- Dwell time
- Time spent on individual pages and the site overall
- Page views
- Page views per visitors

And if the metrics Google sees on your site aren't as good as similar sites to yours, then you will be ranked lower.

Brand signals

Trust is becoming more and more important online. With fake news becoming a big problem on the internet, trust and authenticity is extremely important, so Google tries to avoid indexing websites which include misinformation. So another factor that Google takes into account is your brand.

Many financial advisers freely admit that unless they are part of a very large advice firm, branding has not been much of a priority. But through posting of regular, high quality, valuable and authentic branded content that people can trust – and through multiple channels, it is entirely possible for small financial advice firms to build a strong brand, even if only in the eyes of Google. Just look at Pete Matthew, Martin Bamford and Catherine Morgan as great examples.

Yoast SEO

For those financial advisers using WordPress as their website platform (and many are), there is a tool called Yoast SEO that can be plugged into your site.

Users report getting great SEO results from Yoast and the good news is that there is a free version. In short it:

- Gets you more visitors from Google and Bing
- Attracts more visitors from social media
- Increases your visitors' and readers' engagement

Yes, SEO can be a tough one to get right, but it's important that someone in your business or wider team takes responsibility for it, because it can make the difference between receiving high volumes of website traffic or none at all.

You will find literally millions of articles and videos on the topic online, some of which go into incredible detail. But what is important is that you at least make yourself aware of its importance and start taking some basic steps.

Play by the Rules

Compliance and Reputation in Adviser Marketing

It's worth spending a moment talking about compliance and LinkedIn/Social Media. This is not exhaustive on how financial advisers should use social media compliantly, but some general points need to be made.

For the avoidance of doubt, I am not a compliance officer, so you will always need to work with your own compliance team for definitive guidance.

However, I have met and worked with thousands of financial advisers, some of whom are heavy internet marketing and social media users and who between them have posted tens of thousands of tweets, articles, blogs, podcasts, videos and status updates with little, if any intervention from their compliance people.

I am conscious though, that different financial adviser firms have very different approaches to compliance, with some not allowing their IFAs and advisers to even tweet about football results, right through to those who barely look at any social media posts throughout the year.

There isn't a right or wrong way to handle this topic, but we seem to be getting to a point where the most forward-thinking compliance teams allow advisers to post pretty well whatever they wish on social media within certain ground rules, and with random sample checks taking place once a quarter or every six months.

Those ground rules tend to be:

1. Do not post financial promotions on social media
2. Do not give financial advice on social media
3. Do not bring the business into disrepute on social media

Do not post financial promotions

In fact, you ***can*** post financial promotions on social media – as long as they go through your normal compliance process. But just don't, because no-one wants to see them in their social media feeds anyway. All they do is to reinforce the old perceptions that financial advisers are little more than salespeople.

Do not give financial advice on social media

This is a no-brainer; just don't do it. But generic financial *education* is a very different thing, and in many ways is the backbone of great content posted by many of the most successful financial advisers who use social media.

Do not bring the business into disrepute

We've all seen how easy it is for some people to get into arguments on social media, regardless of the topic being discussed. It's not pretty and can do untold damage to a financial advice business, so keep it professional.

Speaking of keeping it professional, I would like to add one further ground rule based on my own observations of many financial advisers' use of social media over the last fifteen years and how they can impact the reputation of everyone:

Do not bring the wider *profession* into disrepute

I've been working with financial advisers and their use of social media since 2004, and whilst the majority are very professional in their use of it, there is still a sizeable group of financial advisers whose use of online communications is anything but.

I am consistently shocked at how rude and discourteous some advisers are to each other online, and who have no room or respect for other advisers' views and business models.

Many of these comments are made in open forums, on blog posts, twitter and on news websites and do absolutely nothing to enhance the perception and reputation of the profession to the outside world.

Only a couple of days ago I saw an adviser in an online forum ask what one thing the profession needed to do to make itself more appealing to consumers. There were some great answers, all of which were perfectly valid (better marketing, consumer education etc.), but one person suggested that some advisers should think carefully about how they personally portray the profession to the outside world when engaging with their peers. The advice was given that if you see other advisers letting themselves and the wider profession down, don't be afraid to call them out, and when you do, you will usually get a great deal of support from others.

The Dream 100

Affiliate Partners

If you have ever read *The Ultimate Sales Machine* by Chet Holmes, you will have heard of *The Dream 100* concept and it is one that can be applied to ambitious financial advice businesses. It is also an approach used by many high-profile entrepreneurs, including the founder of ClickFunnels Russell Brunson who utilised it to both launch his business and scale it dramatically.

In essence, the Dream 100 is a long-term strategic relationship building campaign where you seek to build real, authentic relationships with people who are a perfect fit for your business – though not as potential clients themselves, though in time that may happen. These are people who are going to help you attract clients or fulfil other planned objectives in your business.

In many ways the Dream 100 concept pulls together a lot of the ideas presented in this book into one single strategy.

You can use the Dream 100 to identify people and organisations who can give exposure to your business or to find people who will either promote your services or introduce clients to you.

We all know that building relationships is important, but this approach should be treated as a mindset. So what we are talking about is building relationships at a far deeper level than we have thus far. If you work with professional introducers this approach could significantly add to your existing relationships.

The starting point is to identify your ideal partners. This could be up to one hundred people, but even ten would work extremely well for a financial advice business. But you have to start somewhere, so let's aim for just one to get us going and then build from there.

So, we are looking for people who have the ability to promote you, your business and services, your events and initiatives and to drive traffic to your website. Ideally, we need people who share similar values and beliefs as yourself and so have the potential to influence our ideal clients (or who could help us to achieve other business objectives). Your Dream 100 could be made up from any of the following as examples:

- Other local business owners
- High profile executives in larger companies
- High profile entrepreneurs
- Journalists
- Writers and authors
- Bloggers and Video bloggers
- Podcasters
- People with large social media followings
- People with small but niche social media followings
- Influencers
- Actors and comedians
- Musicians and celebrities
- Highly influential existing clients
- And so on.

In many ways they could *all* be labelled as 'Influencers' and what is important to note is that you won't necessarily know these people. You may know *of* them but never have met them. So the first step is to make a list of who you would like on your Dream 100 list, but as mentioned earlier let's start with just ten people.

Remember too that your Dream 100 list need not just be people who are spread across the list above, they could *all* be (say) writers at high profile online and traditional newspapers, so think carefully if there is also a specific *type* of influencer that you want to focus on the most.

Create your list

Just for fun, have your first stab at this right now:

1.

2.

3.

4.

5.

6.

7.

8.

9.

10.

For sake of argument, maybe you want to develop a niche in financial planning for sports people, so it would be a good idea to have someone like former Olympic athlete Kriss Akabusi MBE on your list.

You might also want to include a sports journalist on your list, so perhaps add Clare Balding or Eddie Butler.

The people on your list do not need to be famous, but they do need to have some influence – and that influence can be local, online, within a business or in some other sphere. Think also about people within the financial advice profession; there are plenty of high-profile individuals who are not direct competitors.

This is a powerful strategy, but it doesn't happen overnight, so take your time coming up with a list. Hopefully you have already been able to come up with a few.

Do your research

Next, prepare your ground for building the relationships by brainstorming different ideas to get their attention. This means looking for ways to provide value so they become interested in you. This will mean doing your research and this might take some time – hence this being a longer-term strategy.

You will need to find out about things such as their business interests past and present, books they may have written, projects and charities that they have been involved with and hobbies, pastimes and passions. Other than their website, you need to find as reliable sources of information as possible, so Wikipedia will often be useful, particularly if they are in the public eye.

Start to build rapport

The next step is to carefully try to build rapport so that you gradually attract their attention. For the avoidance of doubt, this does not mean stalking them. It means taking an extremely professional approach, but it can be done in a planned, consistent and deliberate manner

An obvious first step is to engage with their social media content. Some of these people will be highly prolific on their chosen social platforms, while others less so. Your aim is to first subscribe to their posts or follow them, and ideally create alerts for their content so that you see all of them. For example, when you follow someone on Twitter, you can also choose to receive a notification each time they tweet.

Alternatively, use a monitoring tool such as Tweetdeck where you can create a column for each person on your Dream 100 list.

You should not engage with every single post they make on social media; that would just be creepy. This is a serious relationship building strategy and if you over do it, the exact opposite will happen. You need to be professional and circumspect, and Like, Comment and Share/Retweet with discretion.

The next step is to occasionally send a direct message that makes a point like,

"Hi John, I saw your tweet/post about leadership and it really resonated with me – thank you. Sarah Jones"

Or,

"Hi John, I saw your tweet/post about leadership and it really got my attention. It reminded me of John Smith's excellent book on the subject – have you read it? Sarah Jones"

Or perhaps,

"Hi John, I saw your blog about leadership today and it really struck a chord. I've forwarded it onto my team. Thanks again. Sarah Jones"

Do you notice the tone of these messages? They are respectful and show the person that they have had an impact on you. Remember, you don't do this on every single post; you need to gauge how often you interact with them for yourself, taking into accounts factors such as the frequency of their posts.

I would suggest taking this approach for three months, which will be long enough for them to have noticed you and for them to feel that you are genuine in your remarks and approach.

There are other things you can and should do. For example, if they have written a book, buy it - purchasing their products is always a good move. It shows that you are serious and at some point you can post your own content – tweet, video, blog etc., which reviews or highlights it – remembering of course to tag them in your comments. Perhaps purchase multiple copies to give away to clients or friends, and then again subtly find a way to let them know. You could always write them a letter via their publisher.

I can't stress enough how important it is to remain professional in all of this. This is not about spamming their twitter feed or coming over as a stalker – this is a genuine attempt to build a relationship. By engaging with them through Likes, sharing, comments and making purchases you are aiming to build rapport, so that when the opportunity comes up to potentially talk to them or meet them, you need to be prepared.

Take the relationship a stage further by using your platform

The next step is to engage deeper with them. And for those of you who have been following this book, you will now see one of the reasons why having your own platform such as a podcast, YouTube channel or online group/community is extremely important. You will now offer that platform to them as a vehicle to promote themselves, highlight an initiative or share their knowledge, expertise and thinking.

Do you remember I mentioned the Financial Adviser Mastermind & Challenge earlier?

The platform I have is a captive audience of financial advisers in our LifeTalk group, and each of the thirty experts I interviewed for the project was given use of LifeTalk as a means to share their expertise. When we were planning the initiative, I created a list of about a hundred people I wanted to interview, but I knew that the people who would accept my invitations were only going to be those with whom I had been working on a relationship – in some cases over several years.

And as you may know, we had some stellar interviews – yes, including Kriss Akabusi. Kriss is one of the UK's top motivational speakers and doesn't come cheap, but because I had taken the time to foster the relationship, he was happy to take part for free. To add to our offer to Kriss, we promised him considerable promotion within our adviser community, a copy of the video, an audio copy and a written transcription which we sent him.

Someone like Kriss doesn't actually need such publicity, promotion or a copy of the video – he has all the video he will ever need after his amazing career as a world class athlete, but most people, whoever they are, respond positively to others who make the effort to build 'proper' relationships.

The reciprocation element is important at this stage of the relationship. Offering copies of your video or podcast with them are used typically when building Dream 100 relationships, but you should also think of other ways that you can help them, because exchange of value is critical.

You could for example offer them some training on a topic or area in which you have expertise and specialise - or even **offer them your service or product for free**. Remember the items on your value ladder from earlier? This is where they could come in handy as gifts – your course, your seminar or your book/eBook.

In short, leverage your platform by offering people on your list the opportunity to use it in a way that will help them.

Gifts and value

I want to stress again that whilst you may have now got the point where you have established content and started to build a relationship, you need to keep the plates spinning from here on if you want to get to the point where they freely refer people to you.

So at this stage, your Dream 100 or Dream 10 people are no longer 'targets' but more like partners – and remember, partners invariably share similar values and beliefs to you. You have:

- Identified your list
- Got their attention by engaging with their content
- Occasionally engaged directly with them
- Offered them access to your platform
- Reciprocated with value

Now is not the time to stop engaging with them, but we don't want to take advantage of the new relationship, so we need to stay professional at all times. So you should continue to engage with their content online through Likes, shares, comments etc. and occasionally send them emails and even letters – just as you would with clients.

At this point, exponents of The Dream 100 approach suggest sending a gift in the mail. "Lumpy Mail" as it is known. In fact, they often suggest sending gifts during the earlier online engagement phase. I know for a fact that many advisers in the UK will find this a little awkward or slightly sycophantic, so it's up to you as to how early you send them a gift in the post. However, whenever you send a gift, it will get their attention, but in my view it is better to send it after you have established a relationship that you feel comfortable with progressing further. And that could well be after they have been a guest on your podcast or other platform.

What could you send them?

Remember earlier that you asked them if they had read a particular book? Send them a copy. Or send them a copy of your own book. Whatever you send them, try to make it personalised and relevant to the content and relationship that has been established up to that point. Receiving stuff out of the blue is nice, but far more effective if it is relevant to the relationship thus far.

In the next chapter we look at video cards and this would be an ideal thing to include in the package. Russell Brunson took exactly this approach when launching his business, sending personalised video cards to everyone on his Dream 100 list.

Generating referrals from your Dream 100 contacts

By now you will hopefully have established some sort of relationship with people on your list, and often to the extent that you have now exchanged emails, spoken on the phone or Skype/Zoom and possibly met them as well. You will more than likely have connected with each other on LinkedIn if they are businesspeople.

If they are on LinkedIn, try to differentiate yourself when communicating with them through the platform, so utilise the audio and video messaging facility on the LinkedIn app.

It's now over to you to move the relationship to the point where they are referring people to you and your business. At this point you might want to re-read the earlier chapter on Referrals because it makes some key points on how to make this happen, one of which is this section about the world's top referral coach Bill Cates:

"One of the key things that Bill teaches is that the referral and introduction process should be a *collaborative* event between adviser and client – in that you work together.

This suggests that after you have worked with a client, you do not just sit back and hope for the best that he or she will introduce you. Neither is it as simple as saying at the end of a meeting *"Who do you know who could benefit from my services?"* as many advisers have been taught over the years. It goes much deeper than that.

In short, you need to teach or train clients *how* to recommend you rather than rely or hoping that they will do it. Bill often recommends going through with your client what they might actually say to people in order to make them more confident and deliberate in their introductory discussions."

In the context of your Dream 100, in the paragraphs above, for the word 'client', read 'Dream 100 connection'. In short, you now need to guide them in *how to refer people to you*. Just because you now have a relationship with these people, you are far from being 'blood brothers', so it does not necessarily mean that they will automatically introduce people to you. And for that reason, I once again highly recommend that you read Bill's book *Get More Referrals Now! The Four Cornerstones That Turn Business Relationships into Gold* at https://amzn.to/2FaGixu because it will teach you how to ask for and generate the referrals you really want from your dream connections.

Summary

Clearly the Dream 100 approach is a long-term strategy, but one that can be incredibly powerful because it combines several marketing elements into one. You will also find that once you have got one or two of your dream connections on board, you will find it easier to attract others. In the example of an adviser who niches into financial planning for sports people, if you have one of the cool kids like Kriss Akabusi as a key relationship, you will find it much easier to attract other high-profile sports people or sport-related influencers.

Start small by getting one of the cool kids on board and then leverage that relationship. Let other potential partners know who is already working with you, so they will want to build a relationship with you too.

Referrals expert Bill Cates makes it very clear that if you can devise and implement a powerful referral and introduction strategy, the world is at your feet and **you need never spend another penny on advertising and promotion again**. Most financial advisers already attract some referrals as a result of the great work they do with their clients, but hardly any have a formal documented referral strategy which consistently and unfailingly attracts the very highest quality clients that they ideally want. If they did, then I wouldn't be writing this book.

The Dream 100 concept takes relationship and referral marketing to a whole other level, where when the moment is right, your dream partners will refer you, talk about you, tweet about you, write blogs about you, post links to your website, record videos about you – and much more.

Start your list of partners today, because it is a list that could change your life forever.

Greetings Cards... with a twist

Video Greetings Cards

To finish up, I want to include a fun idea which encapsulates what much of this book is all about – combining traditional proven techniques with modern-day twists.

The humble paper greetings card has been used to send messages since the 15th century, and the world of business hasn't been slow to take advantage. The benefits of using greetings cards in your marketing mix are simple but powerful:

- To say thank you
- To follow up after a meeting or networking event
- To differentiate your communications
- To send small gifts and to make customers feel special
- To make personal connections through handwritten messages
- To strengthen relationships and build loyalty
- To send invitations to events
- To make special offers

One of the key features of marketing with greetings cards is that you create an emotional response in the recipient, similar to when receiving a Birthday Card, and this happens even when it has been sent by a larger company.

You would be forgiven for thinking that in a digital era there is little point in sending communications via old-school paper cards. But that is exactly the point, because digital dominates our lives, consumers, prospects, clients and our professional introducers crave something that feels much more personal.

Greetings cards are tangible; they're something you can hold in your hands, and they don't instantly disappear like online advertisements or when you visit another page on a website. What's more, when used in conjunction with your other marketing – digital or otherwise, you are increasing the likelihood of success.

And it goes without saying that consumers retain physical print marketing longer than digital. Often, they will even pin it up for a period of time.

Yes, everyone receives junk mail, but greetings cards stand out from the rest because they are a curiosity worth opening. What's more people feel a little guilty throwing them away straight away. In short, it's a pleasant and friendly way of saying "Hi" or "Thanks".

If the simple act of sending a card enhances a relationship or helps you to stand out from the crowd, or even bring in revenue, then it is worth the effort. Obviously, you can brand your cards with your logo, and even add a marketing message.

Now, what if we added a modern digital twist that takes this idea into another realm altogether...

Just imagine what it would be like if someone saw your handwritten envelope on their doorstep and opened the card inside to instantly be greeted with a personalised video message from you.

It's only thanks to today's technology that this is now possible where a thin, high quality, full colour, 4.3 inch LCD video screen and speaker can be included within the body of the card which can play messages. So now you can combine all the benefits of sending greetings cards with the benefits of video, and that is a truly powerful mix. You will also find that recipients of your video card will often be so impressed, they will take photos or videos of it and post them on social media.

There is also another type of video card which uses AR (augmented reality), where at first glance it looks like a perfectly normal greetings card, but when you hold your mobile phone camera over the image on the card, it magically comes to life with your video message.

There are a number of different providers of both types of video card, so do your research and shop around for the best ideas and designs for you. They are available in the UK, but if you are thinking about larger volumes it will probably be better to go to a site such as Alibaba.com where you can source them from China and elsewhere.

Either way, as part of your overall marketing mix, video greetings cards are a powerful and impressive addition. Whether sending one to your clients on their birthday or to invite them to your client event, this will definitely differentiate you from other advisers and will build strong loyalty from them along the way.

And I guarantee it will make them smile...

At the Checkout

Wrapping up

A key point I want to make in this book is this. Yes, it is perfectly possible to attract your ideal clients using any one of the ideas we have talked about, but a robust strategy almost always utilises several tactics simultaneously. But it is vital that you are using tactics that are relevant to your ideal target clients.

Do you know who they are?

Have you created your ideal client avatar where you know and understand what these people look like in excruciating detail?

Are you creating content that is relevant for each of them before you meet them and then after you have met them (hint – it's different)?

And are you creating content that is appropriate for target clients on different platforms?

This last question is one that intrigues me, because it goes back to what I have been talking about at the soft fact questioning stage. Do you know which platforms your ideal clients use to consume content?

Some of them primarily consume content on YouTube, with others mostly listening to podcasts. There will be others who spend most of their online time reading blogs and others who can't stay off Facebook or LinkedIn.

Have you taken the time to get this data from your clients? When you do, it will tell you a lot about where the focus of your marketing should be, and as I always say in my workshops, a great outcome for many IFAs will be to know which online or digital tools they ***don't*** need to use (at least for now).

Knowing your numbers has been a consistent theme throughout this book, from your website to your LinkedIn profile – but also numbers about where and when your ideal clients (and Dream 100 connections) spend their time. If your research tells you that most of your clients read blogs, then there is a big clue as to where you should be putting in your effort, and from there you have the potential to dominate online conversations around your area of expertise or target market.

Who do you think dominates conversations around financial planning in the USA amongst professional and amateur Bass fishermen?

Yes, Jared Reynolds CFP® (see the chapter on golf clinics and niche interests). Jared knows his target market inside out and back to front, so his strategy is to be visible wherever they are.

Back in the day when we started our online community for financial advisers, we had members joining our forums, but multiple other advisers who followed us on LinkedIn or Twitter. When we ran the numbers we discovered that there was very little overlap between those on our site and those who followed us elsewhere, meaning that everyone loved our content, but some preferred to consume it on the site, with others preferring to consume it in a different format on Twitter, Facebook or LinkedIn.

I can't stress enough how important it is to know where your clients hang out in the real world but also in the online world – and then create relevant content for them to consume in those different places.

That's another reason why seminars are so powerful, because many people don't use Twitter or social media – but they *love* a live event.

That's another reason why local sponsorship can be so powerful, because their social life is not online but at the tennis, golf or bowling club, or local arts centre.

And that's another reason why being on the radio or writing articles in newspapers can be so effective because traditional media is what they love most.

Do you see how important this is?

If you don't know your numbers and easily obtained information about your clients and dream connections, then it will become extremely hard to make yourself heard and your marketing effective.

Managing expectations and moving forward

There is a lot of content in this book, with the best part of 100 different marketing ideas and concepts. Some of them won't be new to you, and there will be others that you have tried and given up in the past. I believe that I've shed new light on some of these for you and that they can be used again with some tweaking and strategic thinking.

But there was a small phrase that I've used three times in this book, which may have passed you by along the way – and that is the importance of testing and split testing.

For all your knowledge of numbers, ideal client avatars and market research, great marketing of products and services often involves a lot of trial and error; trying something out, getting feedback and then trying again. It's a bit like fly fishing where you are constantly throwing out your fly or bait, reeling it in and then repeating over and over again until you get a bite. How many fly fishermen and women do you see give up after just one cast? None.

But that's exactly what I see a lot of financial advisers doing. Time and time again I hear them saying *"We tried seminars a few years ago and it didn't work"* or *"Facebook was a waste of time for our advisers"* or *"We gave blogging a go, but nothing came of it"*.

It may well have been that seminars, Facebook and blogging were indeed not the right routes for them to go, but more often than not they didn't produce results because they didn't commit to using these approaches – and *commitment* also means using trial and error and testing what works and what doesn't. It often also means that the bait you put out there wasn't attractive or compelling enough. Your bait, aka your offer, is everything in marketing.

A lot of financial adviser marketing over the years has been about hope. Put up a glossy website and hope that it does something. Blog a few times and hope a great connection reads it. Post an update on LinkedIn and hope people will go to your profile. Do a great job with clients and hope that they will refer you.

Hope isn't a strategy.

Focus is.

If his book has does done anything, it will be to have encouraged you to think much more strategically about where you put your marketing efforts and to get far greater focus on what the right things are to do that will make your proposition **irresistible** to your target clients.

Set the bar much higher and aim to be irresistible to your ideal clients, so they see no other option but to talk to you and only you.

PS

Postscript

So, while we're on the subject of being irresistible to prospects, it's important that we take a look at an old-school sales and marketing methodology and see if it has relevance to today's social media world. I think it does.

Forty-two years ago I was starting out as a Trainee Inspector (the equivalent of today's Broker Consultant), learning the ropes and meeting financial advisers on a daily basis. I was shadowing Dennis who was an extremely experienced and successful Senior Inspector, and we had arrived for a meeting at the offices of a large financial advice and insurance broking firm in the City of London. We signed in (no security passes back then) and the friendly receptionist said *"Take a seat gentleman, and I'll tell them you're here. Would you like some coffee?"*

At the ripe old age of eighteen I smiled to myself, feeling pretty important that I was being offered coffee by some big shots in the City. I moved over to a group of large, comfortable-looking leather armchairs in the corner of the reception area, picked up a copy of a glossy magazine and made myself comfortable.

"Get off your backside Philip! Always stand in reception areas. Never sit." barked Dennis.

Dennis was a Senior Inspector and had been doing the job for at least ten years; he was very successful and looked the part too - wearing the most immaculate suit and tie. Though the fact that he also wore Dr Martens boots with his suit was a detail I never fully understood.

My face flushed red and I jumped to my feet at his command, feeling more than a little embarrassed. The receptionist gave me a cheery wink.

"Sales and marketing is about presence and charisma Philip" continued Dennis – something he had by the bucket load. He was at least six feet four inches and towered over me. Helped of course by his boots.

"When you meet someone for the first time, if you are sitting in their reception area, they subconsciously already have the upper hand. From now on, never ever sit in a reception area again – however long you have to wait."

"Yes Dennis", said I. And I've never forgotten it.

That meeting was in September 1978. Early in January 2020 I arrived for a meeting at the same office block in the City of London. They are now the offices of a global fund management firm and the reception area is a lot shinier. There was a huge amount of security and I had to have my photo taken and show personal ID before even the prospect of being offered a coffee – though there was still a group of comfortable leather sofas for visitors to relax in before their meetings.

To this day, I remember Dennis' words at every meeting I go to, and it's become a 'thing' for me – a sort of ritual before meeting someone for the first time. (It's a bit awkward when meeting people in coffee shops, but hey.) Something has stuck in my head that by standing in a reception area, I will at least be 'on the same level' as the person I'm meeting.

Presence and charisma are indeed important in business – whether meeting people face-to-face or through your online activities, perhaps on video, YouTube, other social media or through expertise-based content that you share with customers and prospects.

Presence is something I also work on when speaking at conferences, though arguably you either have presence or you don't. Can it be trained into salespeople and marketers? Amy Cuddy's excellent book 'Presence' is an essential read if you're interested in the subject.

Sadly, somebody told me that Dennis died a few years ago, but the year that I spent shadowing him taught me some great lessons in sales and marketing. And when I stop to think about the top social media influencers I've met or followed – all of them have radiated and projected presence.

Forty-one years on, my older legs yearn to ease into the opulent armchairs of reception areas at shiny offices in the City, but I have always resisted thanks to Dennis' sage advice.

"People buy people and you never get a second chance to make a first impression" he had added. And he was right.

I wonder how many financial advisers today are missing out on enquires because of the first impression they are creating on their websites and social media?

Quite a few I suspect…

Thank you

We really appreciate you taking the time to purchase and read this book and hope that you have found it valuable. Please help us and consider giving it a five-star review on Amazon because this helps us to spread the word. Thank you.

Interested in purchasing ten or more copies of this book?

Contact us for information on special discounts available for bulk purchases: philip@financialadvice.marketing

Interested in having Philip Calvert speak at your conference, training session or event?

Philip speaks at conferences worldwide, so for an entertaining, high content presentation, training session or keynote speech with actionable takeaways, book Philip today.

Join our Free Private Marketing Forum for Financial Advice Professionals

When you join our marketing and lead generation forum for financial advisers, you'll get free access to fresh strategies for growing and developing your financial advice business and career.

This includes free access to the acclaimed **Financial Adviser Mastermind & Challenge**, an online summit which includes over twenty-four hours of video and audio content and features thirty leading experts to financial advisers such as Carl Richards, Brett Davidson, Michael Kitces, George Kinder, Martin Bamford and many more.

Valued at £997, you can get access free. Request your invitation by sending a message to philip@financialadvice.marketing quoting reference: AMP

Other books for Financial Advisers
by Philip Calvert

Social Media Strategy Planner for Financial Advisers, IFAs, Wealth Managers and Financial Planners

LinkedIn Success for Financial Advisers: Tips, Tricks and Connection Scripts Every Financial Planner Needs to Know

56 New Income Streams for Financial Advisers: How to Turn your Financial Planning Expertise & Experience into Profitable Information Products for the Digital Age

The Financial Planner's Daily Journal: Helping Financial Advisers to Achieve their Goals through Daily Journaling

All available on Amazon.

About the Author

Philip Calvert - Delivering Actionable Ideas to Make a Positive Impact at your Conference, Corporate Event or Sales Meeting.

Philip is an international speaker and author specialising in helping financial advice businesses to market and present themselves with credibility and professionalism through seminars, live events, public speaking, LinkedIn and wider social media.

A world leading authority on LinkedIn and Seminar Selling, Philip speaks worldwide and delivers high value and entertaining keynotes and breakout sessions.

For further information connect with him on LinkedIn at www.linkedin.com/in/saleskeynotespeaker or send an email to philip@financialadvice.marketing.

Visit his website at www.philipcalvert.com

Disclaimer and Terms of Use

This book is provided for research and educational purposes. You do not have resell rights or giveaway rights to any portion of this publication. Only customers that have purchased this publication are authorised to view it. No part of this publication may be transmitted or reproduced in any way without the prior written permission of the author. Violations of this copyright will be enforced in law.

The information services and resources provided in this book are based upon the current internet marketing and economic environment. The techniques presented have been extraordinarily lucrative and rewarding to information marketers, financial advisers and business owners worldwide, however because the internet is constantly changing, some sites and services presented in this book may change, cease or expand with time.

We hope that the skills and knowledge acquired from this book will provide you with the ability to adapt to inevitable internet and marketing evolution. However, we cannot be held responsible for changes that may affect the applicability or effectiveness of these techniques.

Any earnings, income statements or other results quoted, are based on our own and the testing of other marketers and are estimates of what we believe you could earn or achieve. There is no assurance you will do as well as stated in any examples and could be influenced by a variety of factors, not least of which include work ethic and market conditions. If you rely upon any figures provided, you

Printed by Amazon Italia Logistica S.r.l.
Torrazza Piemonte (TO), Italy

13675757R00223